LONDON

A PICTORIAL CELEBRATION

Sketchbook

Jim Watson

SURVIVAL BOOKS • LONDON • ENGLAND

Harley Street doorway

Front cover illustration: Tower Bridge and the City
from the Design Museum.
Front endpaper: Trafalgar Square from the London Eye.
Back endpaper: South Bank and The City from the
London Eye.

First published 2011

Survival Books Limited
Office 169, 3 Edgar Buildings
George Street, Bath BA1 2FJ
United Kingdom
Tel: +44 (0) 1935-700060. Fax: +44 (0) 1935-700060
email: info@survivalbooks.net
website: www.survivalbooks.net

British Library Cataloguing in Publication Data
ACIP record for this book is available
from the British Library.
ISBN: 978-1-907339-37-0

Printed and bound in Singapore by Tien Wah Press

CONTENTS

Chelsea Hospital

3

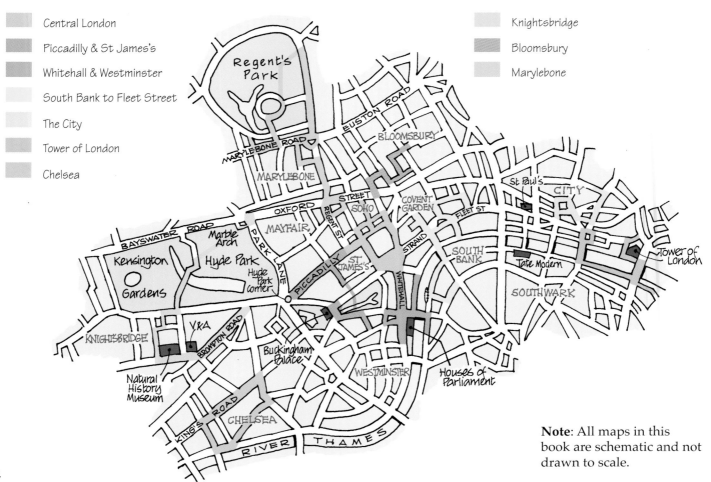

- Central London
- Piccadilly & St James's
- Whitehall & Westminster
- South Bank to Fleet Street
- The City
- Tower of London
- Chelsea
- Knightsbridge
- Bloomsbury
- Marylebone

Regent's Park

MARYLEBONE ROAD

EUSTON ROAD

BLOOMSBURY

MARYLEBONE

St Paul's

CITY

STREET

OXFORD

MAYFAIR

SOHO

COVENT GARDEN

REGENT ST

FLEET ST

BAYSWATER ROAD

Marble Arch

PARK LANE

Kensington Gardens

Hyde Park

Hyde Park Corner

PICCADILLY

ST JAMES'S

STRAND

SOUTH BANK

WHITEHALL

Tate Modern

Tower of London

SOUTHWARK

V&A

BROMPTON ROAD

Buckingham Palace

WESTMINSTER

Houses of Parliament

KNIGHTSBRIDGE

Natural History Museum

KING'S ROAD

CHELSEA

RIVER THAMES

Note: All maps in this book are schematic and not drawn to scale.

4

INTRODUCTION

London is one of the world's great cities, steeped in two thousand years of history and rich in culture, architecture and agreeable surprises – often just around the corner.

It was a privilege for me to spend summer days walking the routes in this book, enjoying the famous sights while bursting with pride at my capital city. The winter months were spent trying to capture the scenes in line and watercolour. Notes accompanying the illustrations provide some historical background and useful facts and figures.

The suggested walks take in all the famous landmarks which are relatively close to each other, so none of the routes exceed four miles in length. They begin and end at underground stations, the circular walks at the same station.

There are of course many ways to get around London but I find the tube most convenient. It's also exciting to emerge from the underground not sure what you're about to see. You emerge, blinking at the sunlight, and are swept along in a great swell of humanity to perhaps the first sight of an iconic scene you may have previously seen only in a photograph. The scale can be unexpected and oddly moving, the Albert Memorial for example. Or the unexpected intimacy of the great financial edifices gathered around that tiny square in front of the Bank of England. The pleasures of London are many and varied but few are such good value for money as just looking.

You could easily complete all the walks in a week of good weather – believe me, it does happen – anything is possible in London! You'll never be far from a cafe or a pub and one of the delights of the city is to linger awhile and watch the world go by. You'll certainly see people from most parts of the globe.

I do hope you enjoy this book and the scenes that inspired it, and that they give you as much pleasure as they always give me whenever I visit ol' London town.

Jim Watson

Rugby, March 2011

Shop sign, Bloomsbury

CENTRAL LONDON

The city centre can be loosely defined as the area bordered by Trafalgar Square, Piccadilly Circus and Cambridge Circus. Shaftsbury Avenue – theatreland's main artery – and Charing Cross road – noted for bookshops – are usually busy but Trafalgar and Leicester Squares are both good places to walk around, seeing the sights and soaking up the lively atmosphere. Charing Cross is considered to be the centre of London, from where all distances are measured.

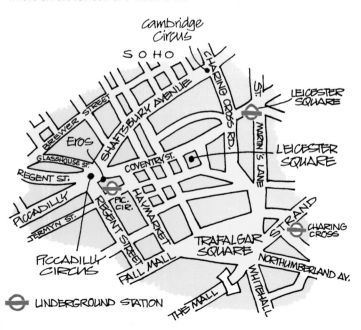

TRAFALGAR SQUARE

Conceived by John Nash and mostly constructed during the 1830s, Trafalgar Square is London's main venue for rallies, outdoor public meetings and celebrations. The square was once famous for its feral pigeons and feeding them was an essential part of the London experience, but with modern 'Health and Safety' concerns, the pigeons – a flock of around 35,000 – were successfully banished using a variety of deterrents including a ban on feeding and the introduction of trained falcons. The result is a much cleaner and more pleasant area to enjoy.

Sir Charles James Napier statue (1855). When Mayor of London, Ken Livingstone expressed a desire to see the two statues of the generals in the square replaced by ones of 'people Londoners would know'.

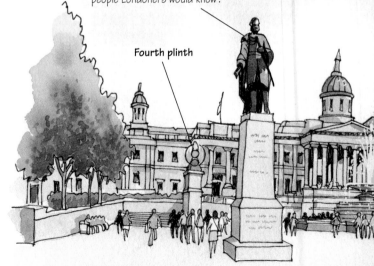

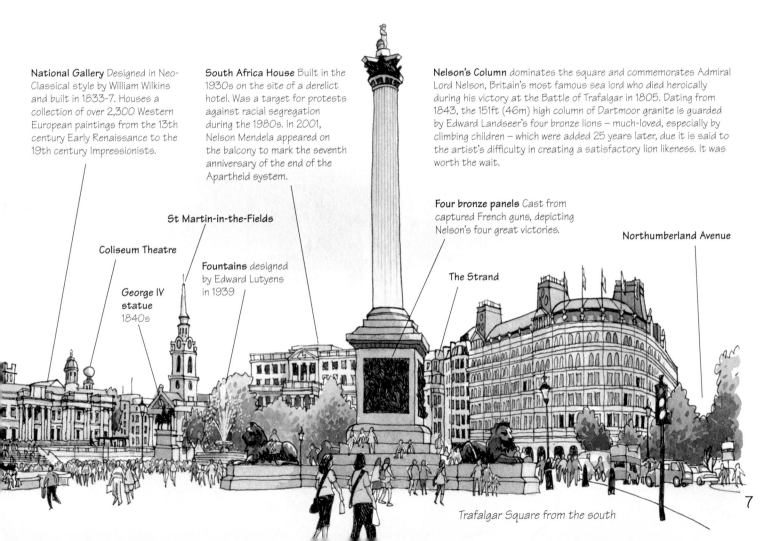

National Gallery Designed in Neo-Classical style by William Wilkins and built in 1833-7. Houses a collection of over 2,300 Western European paintings from the 13th century Early Renaissance to the 19th century Impressionists.

South Africa House Built in the 1930s on the site of a derelict hotel. Was a target for protests against racial segregation during the 1980s. In 2001, Nelson Mendela appeared on the balcony to mark the seventh anniversary of the end of the Apartheid system.

Nelson's Column dominates the square and commemorates Admiral Lord Nelson, Britain's most famous sea lord who died heroically during his victory at the Battle of Trafalgar in 1805. Dating from 1843, the 151ft (46m) high column of Dartmoor granite is guarded by Edward Landseer's four bronze lions – much-loved, especially by climbing children – which were added 25 years later, due it is said to the artist's difficulty in creating a satisfactory lion likeness. It was worth the wait.

St Martin-in-the-Fields

Coliseum Theatre

Four bronze panels Cast from captured French guns, depicting Nelson's four great victories.

Northumberland Avenue

Fountains designed by Edward Lutyens in 1939

George IV statue 1840s

The Strand

Trafalgar Square from the south

7

The mistress of Charles II, Nell Gwynne, is buried at St Martin's, along with the artists William Hogarth and Sir Joshua Reynolds, and the cabinet-maker Thomas Chippendale.

St Martin-in-the-Fields

Admiralty Arch

Latin inscription 'In the tenth year of King Edward VII, to Queen Victoria, from her most grateful citizens, 1910'.

ANNO : DECIMO : EDWARDI : SEPTIMI : REGIS
VICTORIE : REGINÆ : CIVES : GRATISSIMI : MDCCCCX

King Edward VII commissioned Admiralty Arch in memory of his mother, Queen Victoria. Completed in 1912, it's yet another office block – now used by the government – but it effectively cuts off busy Trafalgar Square from the more courtly part of London. Traffic can only use the two outer arches, the central one being reserved for royal processions.

St Martin-in-the-Fields dates to 1726, designed by James Gibbs on the site of an 11th century church. With its rectangular design, portico and baroque steeple, it inspired the design of many colonial churches in America.

Horatio Nelson (1758-1805) was born in Norfolk, England to a clerical family, the sixth of eleven children. He rose rapidly through the Royal Navy ranks and became famous for his exploits during the Napoleanic Wars, losing both his right arm and one of his eyes.

He led a controversial private life, beginning a notorious affair with Emma, Lady Hamilton, while both were married, which continued until his death.

His misfortune with physical injuries continued in the afterlife when his statue was struck by lightning in the 1880s, damaging the left arm. It was repaired in a £420,000 restoration of the column in 2006.

Nelson

The fourth plinth in Trafalgar Square was intended for an equestrian statue of William IV but that was cancelled when the money couldn't be raised, due in part to the king's unpopularity. It's now used to exhibit a series of temporary – and often controversial – works of contemporary art.

Nelson's Ship in a Bottle by Yinka Shonibare occupied the site from May 2010. With sails painted with the artist's trademark patterns, the replica of Nelson's flagship, HMS Victory, was constructed in a perspex bottle large enough for assemblers to work inside.

The 18ft (5.5m) high sandstone statue of Nelson, designed by E.H. Baily, faces south looking towards the Admiralty and Portsmouth where Nelson's & the Royal Navy Flagship HMS Victory is docked. The Mall is on his right flank, where Nelson's ships are represented on the top of each flagpole.

At the south-east side of the square stands a former police box (left), once the smallest in Britain. It was stone-built to last in 1826 and had a phone line installed in 1926, but is no longer in use.

9

LEICESTER SQUARE

One of the capital's most fashionable places to live in the 17th century, with the scientist Isaac Newton and the artists Joshua Reynolds and William Hogarth as residents, Leicester Square is now the pulsating heart of the West End entertainment district. More than 240,000 people pass through it every day, enjoying the bars, restaurants and state-of-the-art cinemas.

The Hippodrome Built in 1900 as a venue for circus and variety acts. In 1985, the building was converted to a classy cabaret restaurant, The Talk of the Town, where the biggest UK and USA acts appeared. It later became a nightclub, opened by Peter Stringfellow in 1983. At the end of 2011, after a £15 million refurbishment, it is due to reopen as a casino and world class entertainment and dining facility.

TKTS, half-price theatre ticket booth

Coventry Street

A bronze statue of the silent film legend Charlie Chaplin wearing his iconic tramp outfit was unveiled in the square in 1981. Born in London in 1889, Chaplin found fame in the USA during the early 1900s. He died in Switzerland in 1977.

The Odeon, built in 1937 and now the largest single screen cinema in the UK, dominates the east side of the square and with a capacity of 1,683, hosts most of London's big film premieres.

The Empire on the north side, originally built as a theatre, has 1,330 seats in the main cinema with eight smaller screens.

A 19th century statue of William Shakespeare surrounded by dolphins stands in a small park at the centre of the square. As the Bard gazes pensively over the glittering film premieres, we can only guess at what he would have made of the A-Team.

Leicester Square

11

CAMBRIDGE CIRCUS

A busy traffic intersection at the junction of Shaftsbury Avenue and Charing Cross Road, Cambridge Circus is dominated by the red-brick Palace Theatre, built in the 1880s by Richard D'Oyly Carte who hoped it would become the home of English Grand Opera. It's now a favourite venue for modern musicals; Les Misérables ran here from 1985 for a record-breaking nineteen years. Andrew Lloyd Webber bought the theatre in 1983 and began a radical restoration in 2004.

'Bugbugs' rickshaws and pedicabs, established in 1998, are now a colourful part of the capital's streetscape.

The Spice of Life pub A Soho landmark and a leading live music venue. Past acts include Bob Dylan, Cat Stevens, Paul Simon, the Sex Pistols and Jamie Cullen.

Prince Edward Theatre

The Cambridge

Palace Theatre

Cambridge Circus and the Moor Street entrance to Soho

Gielgud Theatre, Shaftsbury Avenue

Queen's Theatre, Shaftsbury Avenue

Coliseum Theatre Home of the English national Opera since 1974. Opened in 1904, designed by Frank Matcham, who also designed the Palladium.

St Martin-in-the Fields

Duke of York theatre

St Martin's Lane

Built in the 19th century as part of a slum clearance measure, Shaftsbury Avenue links Cambridge Circus with Piccadilly Circus. It's generally considered to be the heart of the West End theatre district with the Lyric, Apollo, Gielgud and Queen's theatres clustered together on the north side of the street.

Chinese businesses thrive along the Avenue, including restaurants, supermarkets, Chinese banks and mobile phone outlets.

The singer and songwriter, Cat Stevens, was born in Shaftsbury Avenue and the street was a location for the *Harry Potter and the Deathly Hallows* film.

St Martin's Lane is a pleasant, narrow street running north from Trafalgar Square with a surprising mixture of uses, including theatres, bookshops, antique dealers and high class gentlemen's outfitters.

SOHO

With its sleazy reputation now largely cleaned up, Soho is a lively, cosmopolitan area of narrow streets and alleys, a centre of the theatre and film industry, and a residential area for both rich and poor. Old Compton Street is the heart of the capital's gay community.

John Logie Baird first demonstrated television in his attic workshop at 22 Frith Street in 1925, and during the 1850s **Karl Marx** and his family spent a poverty stricken five years on the top floor of 28 Dean Street, where three of his children died. Despite the death of its founder in 1996, **Ronnie Scott's** famous Jazz club still prospers at 46 Frith Street, albeit with a radical makeover in 2006.

Chinatown, around Gerrard Street, is the largest Chinese community in Europe

The Three Greyhounds, Old Compton Street

14

St Anne's church tower All that remains of the original building after a bomb destroyed the rest of it in 1940. A rebuilt church was opened in 1991.

Romilly Street

The French House bar and restaurant in Dean Street was originally a 19th century gin parlour and latterly – with The Coach and Horses – one of the favourite watering holes for most of London's Bohemian writers, actors, artists and musicians.

Gatehouse in Soho Square garden

The Coach & Horses in Greek Street bills itself as 'the West End's Best Known Pub', renowned for 'London's Rudest Landlord', Norman Balon, who ruled the place with the sharpest of tongues from 1943 until his retirement in 2006. Also famous for where Jeffery Bernard was frequently unwell and for the satirical magazine's Private Eye Lunches, held in a hidden-away restaurant behind the bar.

15

PICCADILLY CIRCUS

London's most famous meeting place, where genteel St James's meets the brash West End and Piccadilly meets Regent Street, built in 1819 as part of John Nash's master plan for a grand processional route through the capital. It's said that if you join the crowds who drape themselves around the steps beneath Eros and wait long enough, someone you know will turn up.

The famous statue tops a memorial fountain, erected in 1892-93 to commemorate Lord Shaftsbury, a Victorian politician and philanthropist. Five major roads meet here and traffic used to circulate around the fountain, but in a redesign in the 1980s it was moved to a large paved area on the south side of the junction.

Piccadilly Circus – from the latin meaning 'circle' – is now a must-visit tourist Mecca, busy day and night, and probably most famous for simply being famous.

Piccadilly

Eros

Regent Street

Glasshouse Street

Former Regent Palace Hotel Currently being redeveloped as offices and retail outlets

Piccadilly Circus from Coventry Street

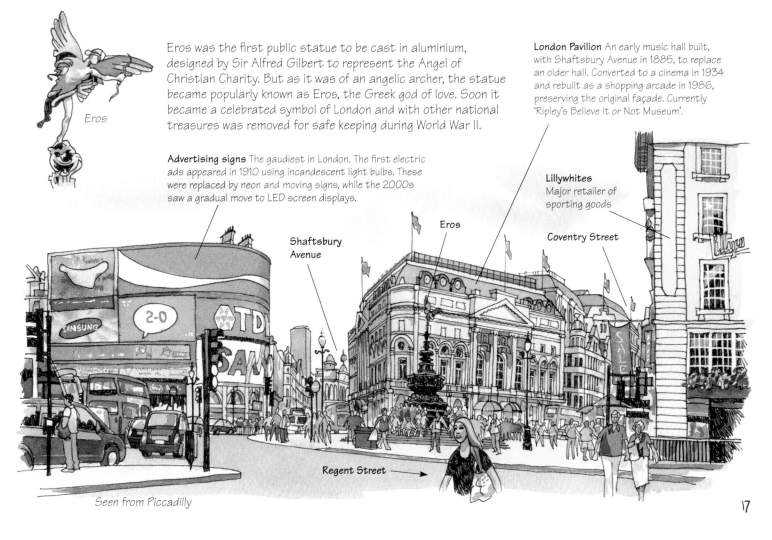

Eros

Eros was the first public statue to be cast in aluminium, designed by Sir Alfred Gilbert to represent the Angel of Christian Charity. But as it was of an angelic archer, the statue became popularly known as Eros, the Greek god of love. Soon it became a celebrated symbol of London and with other national treasures was removed for safe keeping during World War II.

London Pavilion An early music hall built, with Shaftsbury Avenue in 1885, to replace an older hall. Converted to a cinema in 1934 and rebuilt as a shopping arcade in 1986, preserving the original façade. Currently 'Ripley's Believe it or Not Museum'.

Advertising signs The gaudiest in London. The first electric ads appeared in 1910 using incandescent light bulbs. These were replaced by neon and moving signs, while the 2000s saw a gradual move to LED screen displays.

Lillywhites Major retailer of sporting goods

Eros

Shaftsbury Avenue

Coventry Street

Regent Street

Seen from Piccadilly

17

PICCADILLY & ST JAMES'S

The main artery of the West End and one of the straightest and widest streets in London, Piccadilly was once called Portugal Street. Its present name came from the starched collars, or 'pickadills', which were sold in the area and worn by 17th century dandies.

De Beers
Upmarket jewellery store

Colette House
Apartments & offices

Burlington Arcade

Royal Academy of Arts

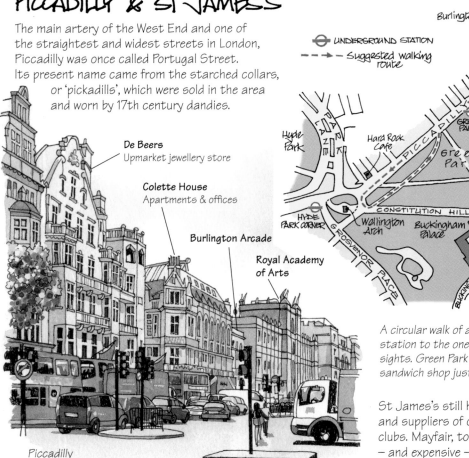

Piccadilly

Ⓣ UNDERGROUND STATION

- - → – Suggested walking route

A circular walk of around three miles from Piccadilly Circus tube station to the one at St James's Park takes in most of the famous sights. Green Park is a good place to take a rest and there's a handy sandwich shop just across the road from the Ritz.

St James's still has the refined atmosphere of royal residences and suppliers of court, with many fine buildings and gentlemen's clubs. Mayfair, to the north of the area, is the most fashionable – and expensive – address in London.

PICCADILLY

Sculptural exhibits in the courtyard

The Royal Academy of Arts is located in Burlington House, a rare example of a surviving grand mansion on Piccadilly. It was originally built in the 1660s, remodelled in the Palladian style for the Earl of Burlington during 1715-17 and greatly enlarged in the 1860s when the RA and five other learned institutions moved in.

The famous summer exhibition of the RA has been held annually for over 200 years and comprises around 1,200 new works by both established and unknown artists submitted for jury selection.

Sir Joshua Reynolds' statue Reynolds (1723-92) was an influential portrait painter. With Thomas Gainsborough he established the RA and in 1768 was elected its first president.

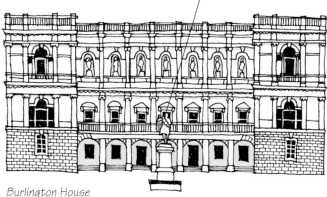

Burlington House

The gatehouse to the Royal Academy of Arts courtyard

19

Piccadilly Arcade

Royal Arcade, Old Bond Street

Burlington Arcade

Shoeshine in
Burlington Arcade

Piccadilly still has four 19th century arcades of small shops selling traditional British luxuries. The Princes and Piccadilly Arcades are on the south side of the street and the Royal Arcade is off Pall Mall. The most famous of the four is the Burlington, built for Lord Cavendish in 1819 to reputedly stop rubbish being thrown into his garden. To further the establishment of order, he recruited beadles (guards) from his own regiment to ensure that his wife and her friends could shop without being molested. Top-hatted and uniformed, beadles still patrol the arcade and have the authority to eject anyone who sings, whistles, runs or opens an umbrella. Modern shopping malls are not expected to follow suit.

Opened in 1797, Hatchards is the oldest bookshop in London and a well-loved institution. Apart from a huge collection of books spread over five floors, Hatchards is also renowned for its celebrity book signings and comfortable atmosphere of armchairs in alcoves and staff who don't rush you. Regular customers have included Lord Byron, the Duke of Wellington, Thackeray, Disraeli, Oscar Wilde and Lloyd George.

Fortnum and Mason is often cheekily dubbed 'the Queen's grocer', but the royal connection was established at its foundation in 1707 by William Fortnum, a footman to Queen Anne, and his landlord Hugh Mason. That original grocery store has grown to today's expansive emporium, recognised internationally for high quality goods and as an iconic symbol of Britain. The firm's handsome Neo-Georgian premises were built in !926-7 and were extended along Piccadilly in a £24 million refurbishment in 2007. Fortnum and Mason has a celebrated tea shop and is famed for its food hampers which can cost up to £25,000 – depending on the extent of luxury you're prepared to pay for.

An exotic-looking clock was hung above the main entrance of the store in 1964 as a tribute to the company's founders. Every hour, four-foot-high figures of William Fortnum and Hugh Mason emerge and bow to each other, accompanied by chimes and 18th century music.

Hatchards

Fortnum and Mason

West of the Ritz, Piccadilly opens out to the appropriately named Green Park, just one part of the almost unbroken expanse of open land stretching about two and a half miles from Whitehall to Notting Hill.

Covering 47 acres, Green Park consists entirely of wooded meadows and, in contrast to its neighbouring parks, has no lake, no building and only a few monuments. The park slopes gently down to Buckingham Palace and the sounds of military bands taking part in the changing of the guard ceremony drift gently back up the hill.

Hard Rock Cafe building, Piccadilly

Ritz Hotel

Green Park (during alterations to Green Park tube station)

The Ritz opened in 1906, the first steel-framed building in Britain and the first hotel in London to have en suite rooms. Its design was modelled on the grand French hotels of the period, master-minded by the famed Swiss hotelier, César Ritz, who once managed the Savoy. The opulence, service and luxury of the hotel caused a sensation in Victorian London and set the standards for future establishments – so much so that the word 'Ritzy' has become a colloquialism for luxury.

The most important gateway into London for over 200 years and the junction of five major roads, Hyde Park Corner is well-used to heavy traffic and has been called the 'busiest corner in the world'. It was also for a time the Grand Entrance from Buckingham Palace into Hyde Park through Wellington Arch and the Hyde Park Screen in line.

But in 1885, Wellington Arch was moved away from the screen to its present position at the top of Constitution Hill to provide an easier route for traffic, and the Grand Entrance to Hyde Park became no longer so grand. Wellington Arch was originally topped with a equestrian statue of the Duke of Wellington but this was replaced by the current work, *The Angel of Peace descending on the Quadriga of Victory* (1912) by Adrian Jones. Aspley House, the home of the first Duke of Wellington, stands on the north side of the screen.

When Park Lane was widened after the war, the area around the arch became a large traffic island mostly laid to grass. There are a number of war memorials on the island, some of them of 'challenging' modern design.

The Wellington Arch

The classical screen to Hyde Park

St James's Street roof garden

ST JAMES'S

In the 1600's, Charles II gave permission for part of the royal park to be developed as an aristocratic residential area. Thus began St James's, still one of the most exclusive residential and commercial areas in London.

St James's Street slopes elegantly down from Piccadilly to St James's Palace with an air of refinement, tradition and good living. The street has several long-established gentlemen's clubs – notably White's, Boodle's, Brook's, and The Carlton – and some handsome old shop-fronts.

St James's Street

Berry Bros & Rudd wine merchants

Shop sign

Supplier of wine to the royal family since the reign of George III, Berry Bros & Rudd's customers have included Pitt the Younger, Lord Byron and the Aga Khan. Britain's oldest wine and spirit merchant began in 1698 at the same St James's Street premises as today. At the 'Sign of the Coffee Mill', Berry not only supplied the fashionable 18th century 'Coffee Houses' (later to become clubs such as Boodle's and White's) but also began weighing customers on giant coffee scales. The company now sells more than 3,000 brands of wines and spirits worldwide.

James Lock & Co, suppliers of 'Ladies' and Gentlemen's hats and caps' was founded in 1676 when Charles II was on the throne. The famous London bowler originated here and the company also made a hat with an eye shade for Lord Nelson and the plumed hat that the Duke of Wellington wore at Waterloo.

Lock & Co

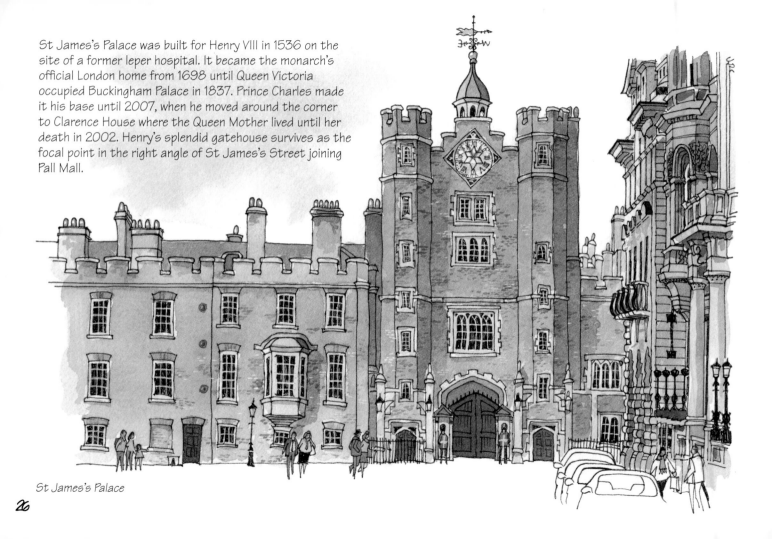

St James's Palace was built for Henry VIII in 1536 on the site of a former leper hospital. It became the monarch's official London home from 1698 until Queen Victoria occupied Buckingham Palace in 1837. Prince Charles made it his base until 2007, when he moved around the corner to Clarence House where the Queen Mother lived until her death in 2002. Henry's splendid gatehouse survives as the focal point in the right angle of St James's Street joining Pall Mall.

St James's Palace

26

Stand on the rather ordinary little footbridge over the lake in St James's Park and two extraordinary views are revealed. To the west Buckingham Palace peeks through the trees and to the east there's an almost fairy tale view of the spires and domes of Whitehall Court and Horse Guards with the towers of the Foreign Office, seen across the willow trees of Duck Island.

The park has a myriad of ducks, geese and coots to enjoy, while winding pathways and clumps of shrubbery all add to an agreeable, garden-like effect.

Buckingham Palace from St James's Park

St James's Park extends to 58 acres and is the oldest of London's royal parks. Then swampy marshland, Henry VIII acquired the area for the Crown in 1532. When James I ascended to the throne in 1603 he had the marsh drained and kept exotic animals here, including camels, crocodiles and an elephant as well as a aviary of exotic birds. Influenced by his time in exile in France, Charles II had the park redesigned in the French style on his return. Further remodelling by John Nash in the 1820s created the park we see today.

Whitehall from St James's Park

BUCKINGHAM PALACE

The official London residence of the British monarch, Buckingham Palace is a setting for state occasions and royal hospitality. It has also been a rallying point for the British people at times of national rejoicing and crisis.

   Originally known as Buckingham House, the building which forms the core of today's palace was a large townhouse built for the Duke of Buckingham in 1705 on a site which had been in private ownership for at least 150 years. It was subsequently acquired by George III in 1761 as a private residence for Queen Charlotte and known as 'The Queen's House'. During the 19th century it was enlarged, principally by architects John Nash and Edward Blore, forming three wings around a central courtyard. The last major structural additions were made in the late 19th and early 20th centuries.

Buckingham Palace became the principal royal residence in 1837, on the accession of Queen Victoria. Widowed in 1861, the grief-stricken Queen withdrew from public life and left Buckingham Palace to live at Windsor Castle, Balmoral Castle, and Osborne House. For many years the palace was seldom used, even neglected. Eventually, public opinion forced her to return to London, though even then she preferred to live elsewhere whenever possible. Court functions were still held at Windsor Castle rather than at the palace, presided over by the sombre Queen habitually dressed in mourning black.

   The palace was seriously damaged during World War II, being bombed seven times. The most serious attack in 1940, destroyed the palace chapel. News film of the damage was shown in cinemas throughout the UK to show the common suffering of both rich and poor.

Buckingham Palace

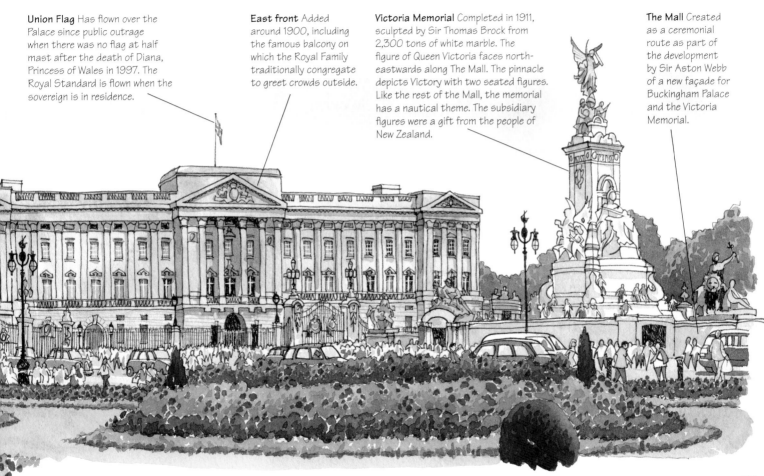

Union Flag Has flown over the Palace since public outrage when there was no flag at half mast after the death of Diana, Princess of Wales in 1997. The Royal Standard is flown when the sovereign is in residence.

East front Added around 1900, including the famous balcony on which the Royal Family traditionally congregate to greet crowds outside.

Victoria Memorial Completed in 1911, sculpted by Sir Thomas Brock from 2,300 tons of white marble. The figure of Queen Victoria faces north-eastwards along The Mall. The pinnacle depicts Victory with two seated figures. Like the rest of the Mall, the memorial has a nautical theme. The subsidiary figures were a gift from the people of New Zealand.

The Mall Created as a ceremonial route as part of the development by Sir Aston Webb of a new façade for Buckingham Palace and the Victoria Memorial.

29

QUEEN ANNE'S GATE

Ministry of Justice (102 Petty France)
Completed in 1976, designed by Sir Basil Spence, who was also responsible for another of London's unlovely buildings, the Household Cavalry Barracks overlooking Hyde Park.

A pretty corner of Queen Anne's Gate is overlooked by the hulking Ministry of Justice

Queen Anne's Gate houses

Close to Westminster, Queen's Anne's Gate is a near perfect early 18th century street of beautiful houses with deep brown brickwork and white porches decorated with finely carved pineapples, foliage and god-like faces. A statue of Queen Anne stands in the street and her ghost is said to walk three times around the street on the night of 31 July, the anniversary of her death. Most of the houses are now occupied by government agencies.

Old Queen Street off Queen Anne's Gate

The Two Chairmen inn sign

The Two Chairmen is an Olde Worlde pub at the Westminster end of Queen Anne's Gate. Rebuilt in 1756, it boasts original oak beams and period fireplaces, and is untainted by modern intrusions such as loud music or TVs. Like many other city centre pubs, the Two Chairmen is closed at weekends when the area is quiet.

The 'two chairmen', immortalised in the pub sign, refers to the two carriers of sedan chairs which could once be hired here. Pub signs originated in 1393 when King Richard II decreed that pubs must have signs so that an inspector could identify and visit the premises to check the quality of the ale. The pictorial sign was developed when the vast majority of the population were illiterate and needed something large, simple and bright to recognise.

The Two Chairmen

WHITEHALL & WESTMINSTER

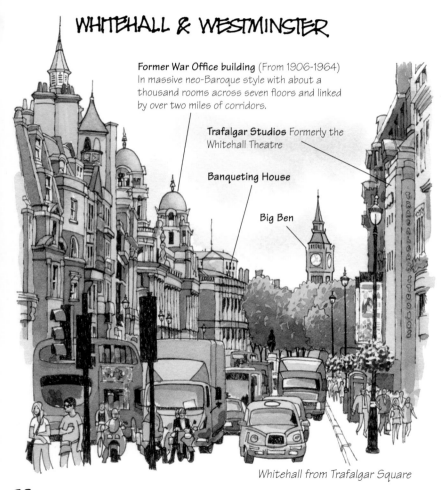

Former War Office building (From 1906-1964)
In massive neo-Baroque style with about a thousand rooms across seven floors and linked by over two miles of corridors.

Trafalgar Studios Formerly the Whitehall Theatre

Banqueting House

Big Ben

Whitehall from Trafalgar Square

Whitehall and Westminster have been at the heart of political and religious power in England for over a thousand years. These days the area is synonymous with government departments, the Civil Service and bureaucracy.

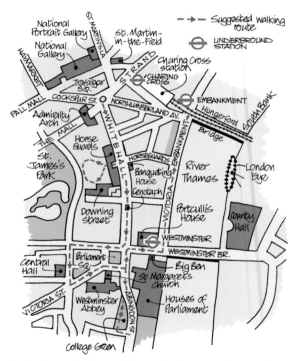

A circular walk of around two miles between Charing Cross and Embankment tube stations.

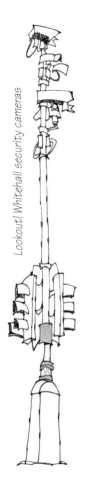

WHITEHALL

Two troopers on black horses in little stone houses guard Horse Guards, a large Palladian style building finished in 1758 to a design by William Kent, which became the headquarters of two major Army commands: the London District and the Household Cavalry. The mounted troopers are popular with tourists, and two others on foot pose for photographs in the courtyard.

The Banqueting House, built in 1622 by Inigo Jones, is one of the few surviving parts of the huge Whitehall Palace, the main residence of English monarchs in London from 1530 to 1698, when it burnt down. Charles I was executed on a scaffold erected outside the building in 1649.

Banqueting House

33

Downing Street was built in the 1680s by Sir George Downing, on the site of a mansion called Hampden House. The Prime Minister, the Chancellor of the Exchequer, and the Chief Whip all have official residences and offices along the short street. For security reasons, iron gates were erected at the Whitehall end in 1989 and public access ended.

No. 10 Downing Street

The Cenotaph, the principal war memorial of Britain, stands in the centre of Whitehall where the annual memorial ceremony is held on Remembrance Sunday in November. In 2005, a striking 'Monument to the Women of World War II' was placed just a short distance northwards from the Cenotaph.

No. 10 Downing Street

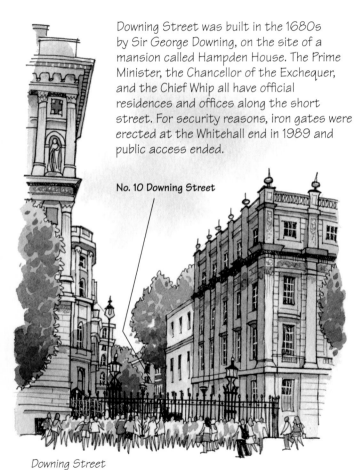

Downing Street

The famous black door of No. 10 opens only from the inside. There are actually two doors, which are exchanged when one needs repainting. Originally black oak, they're now made of blast-proof steel and require eight men to lift each one. The zero of the number '10' is set at a slight angle on the door as a nod to the original number which had a badly-fixed zero.

No. 10 contains some 100 rooms, and after 300 years of London pollution the external brickwork became blackened. The bricks are actually a yellow colour but are now painted black to keep their familiar appearance.

The Cenotaph

Ministry of Defence, Horse Guards Avenue

The northern entrance of 'Main House', headquarters of the MOD, is flanked by two monumental statues, *Earth and Water* by Charles Wheeler. The Neoclassical edifice was built between 1938-59, designed by Vincent Harris to house the Air Ministry and the Board of Trade.

Horse Guards Parade

The annual ceremonies of Trooping the Colour and Beating the Retreat are held on Horse Guards Parade, formerly the Palace of Whitehall's tiltyard where tournaments were held for Henry VIII. It's also the site of the beach volleyball competition of the 2012 Summer Olympics in London.

Once used as a car park, the Parade has been cleared since 1991, after the Provisional IRA launched a mortar shell at Number 10 from a van parked in Whitehall. It exploded in the back garden, blowing out some windows while Prime Minister John Major was holding a Cabinet meeting.

The garden of No 10 Downing Street backs onto Horse Guards Parade

HOUSES OF PARLIAMENT

Since 1512 the Palace of Westminster has been the seat of two houses of the United Kingdom parliament. The Old Palace, a medieval building, was mostly destroyed by fire in 1834. Its replacement, a gothic masterpiece by Charles Barry and Augustus Pugin, who both died during the thirty-year construction, was completed in 1870.

Victoria Tower 323ft (98.5m) high, once the tallest secular building in the world. Houses three million documents of the Parliamentary Archives in almost six miles of steel shelves spread over 12 floors.

Lords' Chamber The lavishly decorated debating area measures 45ft by 80ft (14m by 25m) The benches in the Chamber, as well as other furnishings in the Lords' part of the palace, are coloured red. The upper part of the Chamber is decorated by stained glass windows and by six allegorical frescoes representing religion, chivalry and law.

Central Tower Octagonal in shape and 300ft (92m) tall, stands above the Central Lobby. It's part of the building's ventilation system or as cynics have it, for the removal of hot air.

The Terrace One of the most exclusive dining places in London

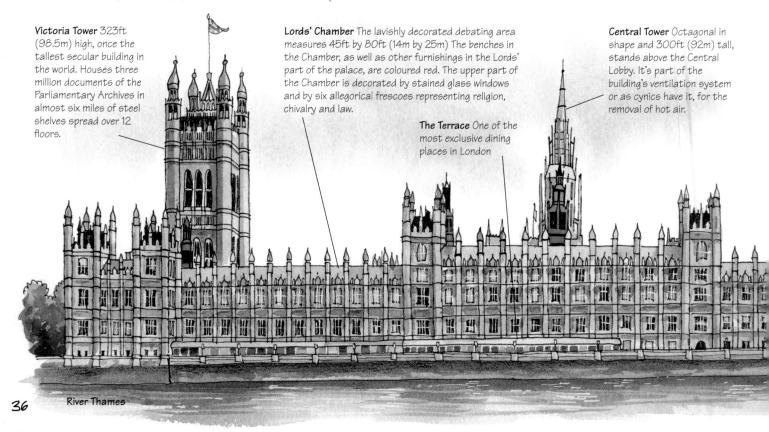

River Thames

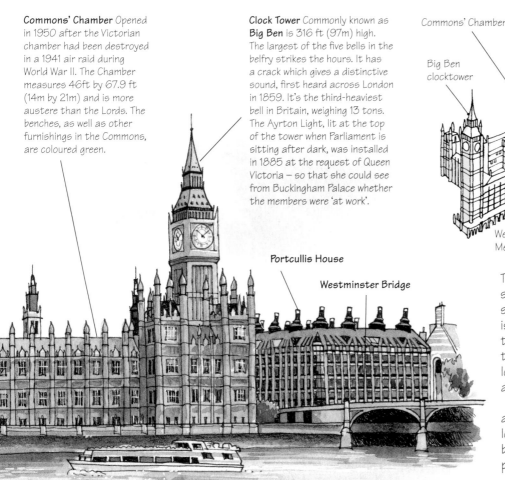

Commons' Chamber Opened in 1950 after the Victorian chamber had been destroyed in a 1941 air raid during World War II. The Chamber measures 46ft by 67.9 ft (14m by 21m) and is more austere than the Lords. The benches, as well as other furnishings in the Commons, are coloured green.

Clock Tower Commonly known as **Big Ben** is 316 ft (97m) high. The largest of the five bells in the belfry strikes the hours. It has a crack which gives a distinctive sound, first heard across London in 1859. It's the third-heaviest bell in Britain, weighing 13 tons. The Ayrton Light, lit at the top of the tower when Parliament is sitting after dark, was installed in 1885 at the request of Queen Victoria – so that she could see from Buckingham Palace whether the members were 'at work'.

Portcullis House

Westminster Bridge

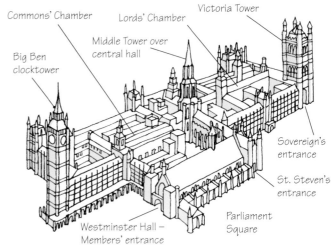

Commons' Chamber

Big Ben clocktower

Lords' Chamber

Middle Tower over central hall

Victoria Tower

Sovereign's entrance

St. Steven's entrance

Parliament Square

Westminster Hall – Members' entrance

The Palace has over 1,100 rooms, 100 staircases and 3 miles of passageways spread over four floors. The ground floor is offices, dining rooms and bars, and the first floor houses the main rooms of the Palace, including debating chambers, lobbies and libraries. Committee rooms and offices are on the two top floors.

The four clock faces are each 23ft (7m) across and each minute hand 14ft (4.3m) long. Accurate timekeeping is maintained by adding or subtracting from a pile of old penny coins on the pendulum.

WESTMINSTER

Portcullis House Britain's most expensive office block, commissioned in 1992 and opened in 2001 to provide offices for 210 Members of Parliament and their staff. The cost was initially estimated to be £165 million but, after building cost inflation and delays, the price increased to £235 million which included £150,000 for decorative fig trees, £2 million for electric blinds and reclining chairs at £440 each.

Westminster tube station was rebuilt at the same time underneath. A thick slab of concrete separates Portcullis House from the station to protect MPs from bomb attack.

Westminster Hall The oldest surviving part of the original Palace of Westminster, built for William II in 1097, then the largest hall in Europe. It has the widest clearspan medieval roof in England, measuring 68ft across by 240ft long (21m by 73m). Charles I, Sir Thomas More and Guy Fawkes were all condemned to death at trials in this hall. It's now mainly used for ceremonial occasions. The bodies of Sir Winston Churchill (1965) and the Queen Mother (2002) are among those of a number of prominent people to lie in state in the hall before their funerals.

Big Ben

Oliver Cromwell statue Hamo Thornycroft's bronze statue was erected amid controversy over public funding in 1899. In 2008, the statue was restored to mark the 350th anniversary of Cromwell's death.

The Treasury

Westminster from Parliament Square

College Green

College Green, a small grass-covered public area across the road from Parliament – actually the roof of an underground car park – is a favourite location for TV crews to present political reports and interview politicians.

The Jewel Tower, off College Green, is another surviving part of the of the medieval royal Palace of Westminster. It was built around 1365 to house the treasures of Edward III and was known as the 'King's Privy Wardrobe'.

Westminster Bridge, opened in 1750, was the first across the Thames since the London Bridge. The present bridge opened in 1862 and was designed to complement the Palace of Westminster. It's painted the same green as the benches in the House of Commons.

Jewel Tower

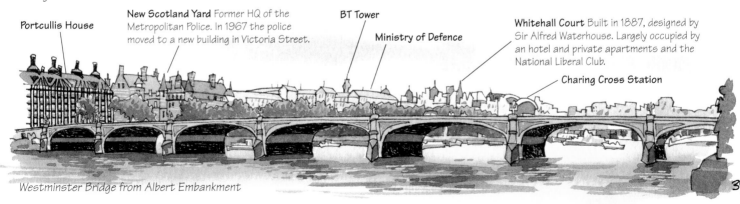

Portcullis House

New Scotland Yard Former HQ of the Metropolitan Police. In 1967 the police moved to a new building in Victoria Street.

BT Tower

Ministry of Defence

Whitehall Court Built in 1887, designed by Sir Alfred Waterhouse. Largely occupied by an hotel and private apartments and the National Liberal Club.

Charing Cross Station

Westminster Bridge from Albert Embankment

WESTMINSTER ABBEY

One of the most famous facades in the world, the twin towers at the western end of Westminster Abbey command attention, but the beautifully decorated Lady Chapel at the Eastern end is equally striking. The Abbey is the largest church in Britain, stretching some 530ft (162m) from end to end. Mainly Gothic in design, it's the traditional venue for coronations and the burial site for British royalty and national heroes.

An abbey has stood on this site since 620. Edward the Confessor began his own 'minster' here, dedicated in 1065, only ten days before Edward himself was interred in the foundations. William the Conquerer was crowned in the Abbey in 1066 setting a precedent for almost every British monarch since. Completed in 1259, the Chapter House has the finest medieval tiled floor in England. The first 'Mother of Parliament' met here from 1257, the origins of the modern House of Commons.

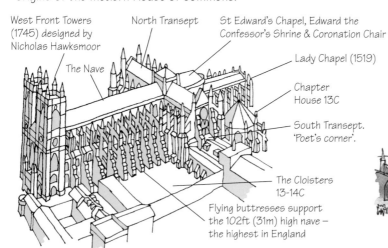

West Front Towers (1745) designed by Nicholas Hawksmoor

North Transept

St Edward's Chapel, Edward the Confessor's Shrine & Coronation Chair

The Nave

Lady Chapel (1519)

Chapter House 13C

South Transept. 'Poet's corner'.

The Cloisters 13-14C

Flying buttresses support the 102ft (31m) high nave – the highest in England

Westminster Abbey

40

Broad Sanctuary (1858), a spectacular Gothic revival building adjacent to Westminster Abbey, was designed by Sir George Gilbert Scott, who was also responsible for other notable London landmarks such as St Pancras station and the Albert Memorial. Scott designed or altered some 800 buildings, including 40 workhouses.

Broad Sanctuary

The simple 'Anglican Church of St Margaret' stands right in the magnificent shadow of Westminster Abbey. Originally founded in the 12th century by Benedictine monks, it became the parish church of the Palace of Westminster in 1614, when the Puritans, unhappy with the highly liturgical Abbey, chose to hold Parliamentary services in the more 'suitable' St Margaret's; a practice that has continued since.

Sir Walter Raleigh, famous for introducing potatoes and tobacco to England, was buried here after being executed for his treasonable part in a plot against King James I. It's also the final resting place of John Milton, the poet.

The church is a popular venue for society weddings. Samuel Pepys and Sir Winston Churchill were married here and all members of the two Houses of Parliament and staff enjoy the same privilege.

St Margaret's

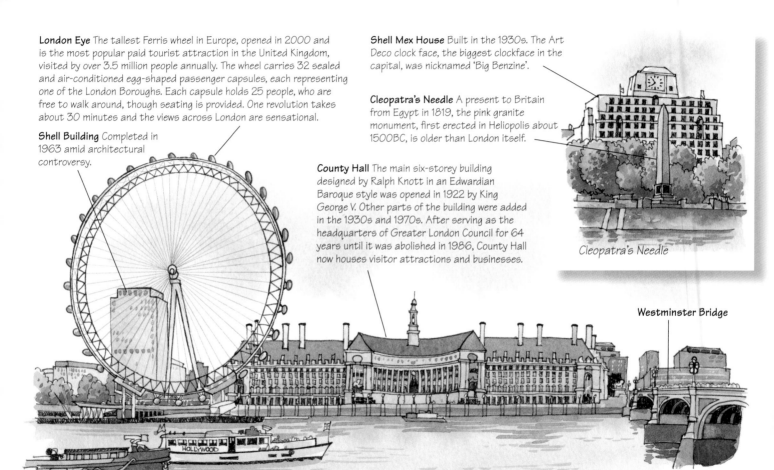

London Eye The tallest Ferris wheel in Europe, opened in 2000 and is the most popular paid tourist attraction in the United Kingdom, visited by over 3.5 million people annually. The wheel carries 32 sealed and air-conditioned egg-shaped passenger capsules, each representing one of the London Boroughs. Each capsule holds 25 people, who are free to walk around, though seating is provided. One revolution takes about 30 minutes and the views across London are sensational.

Shell Building Completed in 1963 amid architectural controversy.

Shell Mex House Built in the 1930s. The Art Deco clock face, the biggest clockface in the capital, was nicknamed 'Big Benzine'.

Cleopatra's Needle A present to Britain from Egypt in 1819, the pink granite monument, first erected in Heliopolis about 1500BC, is older than London itself.

County Hall The main six-storey building designed by Ralph Knott in an Edwardian Baroque style was opened in 1922 by King George V. Other parts of the building were added in the 1930s and 1970s. After serving as the headquarters of Greater London Council for 64 years until it was abolished in 1986, County Hall now houses visitor attractions and businesses.

Cleopatra's Needle

Westminster Bridge

The view across the Thames from Victoria Embankment

Westminster Cathedral, Victoria Street The largest Catholic church in England and Wales, opened in 1903 and designed by John Francis Bentley in a striking pink and white striped Byzantine style. The bell tower is 273ft (83m) high and the nave (60ft /18m) is the widest in England.

Player's Theatre

Charing Cross

Westminster Cathedral

Taxi Driver's Hut where hard-pressed 'cabbies' can enjoy a well-earned rest. Established in 1875 for horse-drawn hansom cab drivers, 13 are still in use around London.

Now the fifth-busiest rail terminal in London, the original Charing Cross railway station was built on the site of the old Hungerford Market in 1864. In 1990 most of the area above the platforms was covered by Embankment Place, a huge post-modern style office and shopping complex. Trains cross Hungerford Bridge over the River Thames serving the south-east of England. Walkways alongside the railway section were opened in 2002.

43

SOUTH BANK TO FLEET STREET

The South Bank is an arts and entertainment area stretching two miles along the south bank of the Thames between the London Eye and the Design Museum.

The southern end was the site of the Festival of Britain in 1951. It's now the location for the National Theatre, the Royal Festival Hall, the Queen Elizabeth Hall and The Hayward Art Gallery. The wooded walks along the Thames Embankment are delightful but the 1950s architecture can be a disappointment.

Lincoln's Inn Field's
Old Curiosity Shop
Bow Street Police Station
Portsmouth St
Sardinia St
Royal Opera House
Covent Garden
Carey St
Law Courts
CHANCERY LANE
FLEET STREET
Prince Henry's Room
Temple Bar
Bush House
Portugal Street
Kingsway
Drury Lane
Bow St.
Long Acre
Wellington St.
Aldwych
St. Paul's Church
Strand
Arundel
TEMPLE
Charing Cross
Savoy Hotel
Cleopatra's Needle
Somerset House
Oxo Tower
National Theatre
Waterloo Br.
River Thames
Hungerford Br.
WHITEHALL
Royal Festival Hall
WATERLOO
London Eye
Waterloo International Station
County Hall

🚇 UNDERGROUND STATION
- → - Suggested walking route

A walk of around 3.25 miles between Waterloo and Temple tube stations. Some gentle hills. Stone steps up to Waterloo bridge.

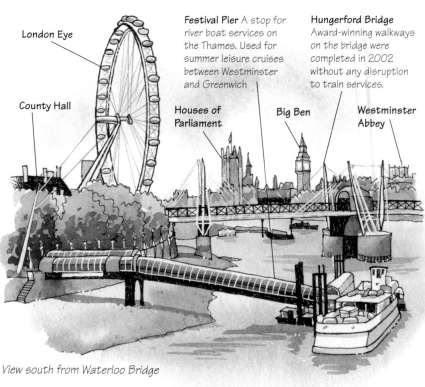

London Eye

County Hall

Festival Pier A stop for river boat services on the Thames. Used for summer leisure cruises between Westminster and Greenwich

Hungerford Bridge Award-winning walkways on the bridge were completed in 2002 without any disruption to train services.

Houses of Parliament

Big Ben

Westminster Abbey

View south from Waterloo Bridge

SOUTH BANK

The National Theatre is one of the United Kingdom's two most prominent publicly funded theatre companies (the other is the Royal Shakespeare Company). The National is housed in a sprawling and much criticised Brutalist architecture building, designed by architects Sir Denys Lasdun and Peter Softley, which has the distinction of appearing in the top ten of both the 'most popular' and 'most hated' London buildings in simultaneous opinion surveys. There are three separate auditoria, the Lyttelton, Cottesloe and Dorfman, which opened individually between 1976 and 1977.

The Oxo Tower

When permission for illuminated signs advertising its product was refused, the manufacturer of Oxo cubes cleverly built a tower with four sets of three vertically-aligned windows, each of which 'coincidentally' happened to be in the shapes of a circle, a cross and a circle.

The National Theatre

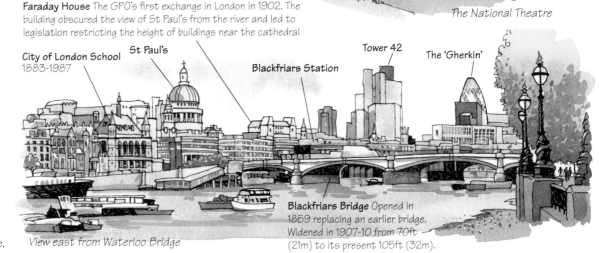

Faraday House The GPO's first exchange in London in 1902. The building obscured the view of St Paul's from the river and led to legislation restricting the height of buildings near the cathedral

City of London School 1883-1987

St Paul's

Blackfriars Station

Tower 42

The 'Gherkin'

Blackfriars Bridge Opened in 1859 replacing an earlier bridge. Widened in 1907-10 from 70ft (21m) to its present 105ft (32m).

View east from Waterloo Bridge

Wellington Street rises unhurriedly from the Strand to Covent Garden with the Lyceum Theatre standing prominently at its foot. There's been a theatre with this name here since 1765. The present one opened in 1834 to a design by Samuel Beazley but fell into disrepair and closed in 1986. It reopened In 1996, restored and reconverted into a venue for large-scale musicals and opera. Since 1999 it has been home to The Lion King, which has grossed over £289 million and been seen by more than eight million people.

'The Wellington' public house

Lyceum Theatre and Wellington Street

Tavistock Street

In medieval times this area was a garden that supplied Westminster Abbey with produce. These days the narrow streets are an attractive blend of small shops, coffee houses and restaurants, and frequently a peaceful antidote to the crowds thronging the central piazza.

COVENT GARDEN

The first theatre on the Royal Opera House site was built in 1732, but it burnt down in 1808 and a subsequent building suffered a similar fate in 1855. The façade, foyer and auditorium of the present Opera House were designed by Edward Barry in 1858, but almost every other part of the complex came from a huge reconstruction in the 1990s. It has been the home of The Royal Opera since 1945, and the Royal Ballet since 1946. Most of the world's greatest singers and dancers have performed on its stage and 'Covent Garden' is today considered to be one of the world's leading opera houses.

The first court in Bow Street, then a notorious gin-soaked area, was established in a private house in 1784. The novelist Henry Fielding, who served as a magistrate, established the 'Bow Street Runners', Britain's first paid police force, to tackle the crime and disorder. The 'official' Magistrates Court building was completed in 1881 and closed in 2006. Famous defendants who appeared there on their way to higher courts include Casanova, Dr Crippen, the Kray twins. General Pinochet and Oscar Wilde.

Floral Hall Part of the old Covent Garden Market. Became part of the Opera House in a radical 1996-99 renovation.

Bow Street Magistrate's Court

'The Young Dancer'
Enzo Piazotta's statue, erected in 1988

Royal Opera House

The Piazza and the portico of St Paul's Church

Covent Garden was originally designed by 17th century architect Inigo Jones to an Italian model, though the fine buildings around today's square are almost entirely Victorian. Charles Fowler's neo-classical covered market building was developed on the site of a former walled garden at the centre of the square in 1833. Further development turned Covent Garden into London's main fruit and vegetable wholesale market.

The Central Market

Designed by inigo Jones, St Paul's Church was consecrated in 1638 and has long been called the 'actors' church'. The main entrance on the square has never been used and access is through a pleasant garden at the west end. The first Punch and Judy show was performed under the portico of St Paul's in 1662 and recorded by Samuel Pepys in his diary.

St Paul's churchyard

By the end of the 1960s, traffic congestion around the area had become a problem and in 1974 the market relocated. The central building re-opened as a shopping centre in 1980, and is now a hugely popular tourist location with cafes, bars, small shops, restaurants and market stalls. There are trendy shops around the square and a procession of street entertainers to enjoy.

 Covent Garden tube station has no escalators, access is by lift only. There's also an emergency spiral staircase of almost 200 steps – the equivalent of climbing a five-storey building.

The Market central hall & restaurant

South entrance to the Central Market

The Central Market from Russell Street

THE STRAND

For many years the only link between the City and Westminster, the Strand was lined with fine buildings and palaces.

The Savoy opened in 1889, Britain's first luxury hotel, built by impresario Richard D'Oyly Carte with profits from his Gilbert and Sullivan operas.

Somerset House dates from 1776–96, the Neoclassical masterpiece of Sir William Chambers and extended by classical Victorian wings to the north and south. There's a display of 55 fountains in the courtyard and each Christmas the area is turned into an open air ice rink.

Savoy Hotel. Closed in 2007 and reopened in 2010 after a £210m refurbishment

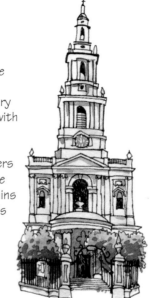

St Mary-le-Strand

St Clement Danes

There are two churches beached on island sites along the Strand.

St Mary-le-Strand was built during 1714-17, the first major project for James Gibbs, who later went on to design St Martin-in-the-Fields.

St Clement Dane was completed in 1682 by Sir Christopher Wren. It's now the central church of the Royal Air Force and claims to be the church featured in the nursery rhyme *Oranges and Lemons*, as the bells play this tune.

Somerset House

The Royal Courts of Justice, commonly called the Law Courts, house the Court of Appeal of England and Wales and the High Court of Justice of England and Wales. They are the nation's main civil courts dealing with cases such as divorce, libel, and appeals. Criminal cases are dealt with at the Old Bailey nearby.

The building is a sprawling and fanciful edifice in Victorian Gothic style designed by George Edmund Street, a solicitor turned architect. It was built in the 1870s and opened by Queen Victoria in December 1882. The Law Courts are said to contain some 1,000 rooms with 3.5 miles of corridors. TV crews and protestors are a familiar sight outside, waiting for verdicts to be delivered.

Temple Bar

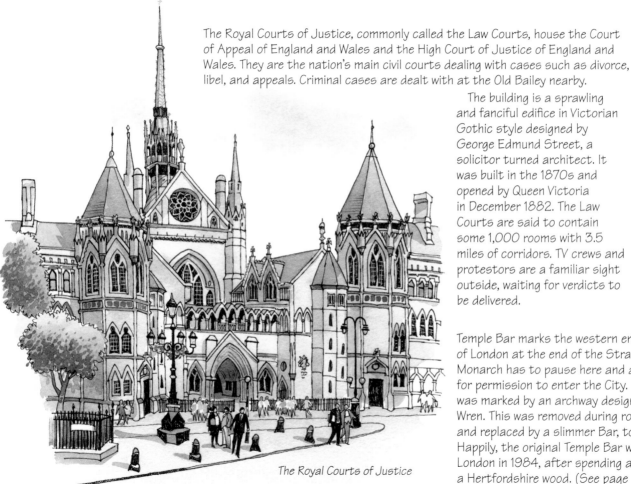

The Royal Courts of Justice

Temple Bar marks the western entrance to the City of London at the end of the Strand. Traditionally, the Monarch has to pause here and ask the Lord Mayor for permission to enter the City. Originally, the Bar was marked by an archway designed by Christopher Wren. This was removed during road widening in 1878 and replaced by a slimmer Bar, topped by a griffin. Happily, the original Temple Bar was returned to London in 1984, after spending around 100 years in a Hertfordshire wood. (See page 62)

FLEET STREET

Despite the last major British news office, Reuters, leaving in 2005, 'Fleet Street' continues to be the byword for the British national press. Fleet Street is now more associated with the law and its inns and barristers' chambers, many of which are down alleys and around courtyards off Fleet Street itself.

No. 186 Fleet Street Where Sweeney Todd, the demon barber of Fleet Street, had his shop. He is alleged to have murdered over 150 customers there and made them fillings for Mrs Lovett's pies. The Victorian melodrama is most probably an urban myth but the story has had numerous TV and film adaptions and inspired a famous musical by Stephen Sondheim.

St Dunstan-in the-West Founded around 1000AD. The present building has stood here since 1831. Its clock was the first on public display in London with a minute hand

Royal Courts of Justice

The Thai Square Restaurant was formerly the famous Wig & Pen Club. Built in 1625, it was the home of the gatekeeper of Temple Bar who began the catering tradition by offering 'a penn'orth' of meat and bread to the crowds who used to gather there.

Of the many slim buildings in Fleet Street, Ye Olde Cock Tavern is the narrowest. It was originally in a building across the street, but after that was bought by a branch of the Bank of England in 1887, the tavern moved lock stock and barrel, to the other side.

Thai Square

Old Cock Tavern

Fleet Street from the Fetter Lane junction

Prince Henry's Room

Old Curiosity Shop

It's unlikely that the Old Curiousity Shop was the one that inspired Charles Dickens to write the novel of the same name, but this is a genuine 17th century building, one that survived the Great Fire of 1666, and probably the oldest shop in central London.

Built in imposing Neo-Classical style as a trade centre by an American, Irving T. Bush, and completed in 1935, Bush House is graced with various statues symbolising Anglo-American relations. Most famous as the headquarters of the BBC World Service, but that is due to move to a new extension of Broadcasting House in 2012.

Built around 1600 as part of a Fleet Street inn, Prince Henry's room refers to the coat of arms and the initials PH in the centre of a fine Jocobean ceiling, probably in honour of James I's eldest son, Henry, who died at the age of 16 before he became King. The beautiful half-timbered house, which escaped the Great Fire, is built over the entrance to the Inner Temple, one of the ancient four Inns of Court (professional associations for barristers and judges) in London.

Bush House

THE CITY

The historic core of the modern conurbation, London's famous 'Square Mile' is now a major business and financial centre rivalling New York City as the heart of global finance. The contrast between the dour, warren-like Victorian buildings and the gleaming new towers is what gives the City its distinctive character.

Mansion House Official residence of the Lord Mayor completed in 1753.

One Poultry Office & retail building opened in 1998. Shaped like a ship, it's one of London's leading post-modern buildings and continues to divide architectural critics.

St Mary-le-Bow

Poultry

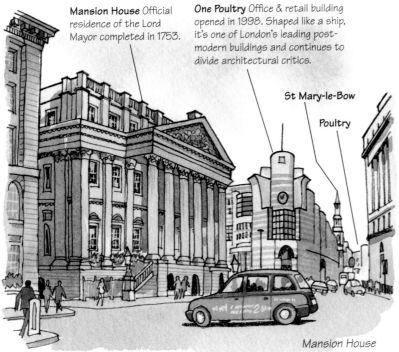

Mansion House

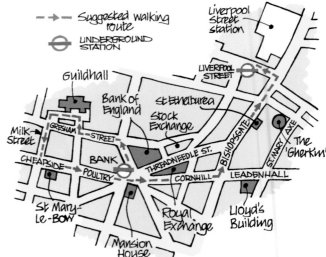

Suggested walking route

UNDERGROUND STATION

Liverpool Street station

LIVERPOOL STREET

Guildhall

Bank of England

St Ethelburea

Stock Exchange

Milk Street

GRESHAM STREET

CHEAPSIDE

BANK

POULTRY

THREADNEEDLE ST.

BISHOPSGATE

ST MARY AXE

The 'Gherkin'

CORNHILL

LEADENHALL

St Mary-le-Bow

Royal Exchange

Lloyd's Building

Mansion House

A walk of around 1.25 miles between Bank and Liverpool tube stations. The City is an interesting place to wander around with many a surprise to discover.

The City – dark suits and an appropriately named tube station: Bank

54

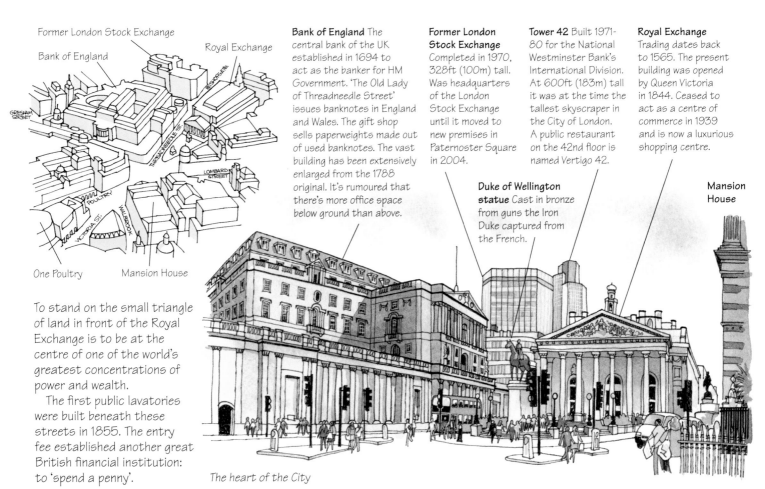

Former London Stock Exchange

Bank of England

Royal Exchange

GRESHAM STREET

THREADNEEDLE ST.

BISHOPSGATE

LOMBARD STREET

POULTRY

VICTORIA ST.

WALBROOK

One Poultry

Mansion House

Bank of England The central bank of the UK established in 1694 to act as the banker for HM Government. 'The Old Lady of Threadneedle Street' issues banknotes in England and Wales. The gift shop sells paperweights made out of used banknotes. The vast building has been extensively enlarged from the 1788 original. It's rumoured that there's more office space below ground than above.

Former London Stock Exchange Completed in 1970, 328ft (100m) tall. Was headquarters of the London Stock Exchange until it moved to new premises in Paternoster Square in 2004.

Tower 42 Built 1971-80 for the National Westminster Bank's International Division. At 600ft (183m) tall it was at the time the tallest skyscraper in the City of London. A public restaurant on the 42nd floor is named Vertigo 42.

Royal Exchange Trading dates back to 1565. The present building was opened by Queen Victoria in 1844. Ceased to act as a centre of commerce in 1939 and is now a luxurious shopping centre.

Duke of Wellington statue Cast in bronze from guns the Iron Duke captured from the French.

Mansion House

To stand on the small triangle of land in front of the Royal Exchange is to be at the centre of one of the world's greatest concentrations of power and wealth.

The first public lavatories were built beneath these streets in 1855. The entry fee established another great British financial institution: to 'spend a penny'.

The heart of the City

55

Traditionally, only those born within the sound of St Mary-le-Bow bells can claim to be true Cockneys.

St Mary-le-Bow

The Guildhall

Sir Christopher Wren famously rebuilt St Mary-le-Bow in 1670-80 after the Great Fire, with one of his characteristic 'wedding cake' steeples. The church was bombed in 1941 leaving only the steeple and two outer walls standing, but was restored in 1951-62.

Dating from 1411, the Guildhall escaped the Great Fire and is thought to have been where citizens came at one time to pay their taxes. The rather quirky building is no longer the headquarters of the Corporation of London and is now used mainly for ceremonial functions.

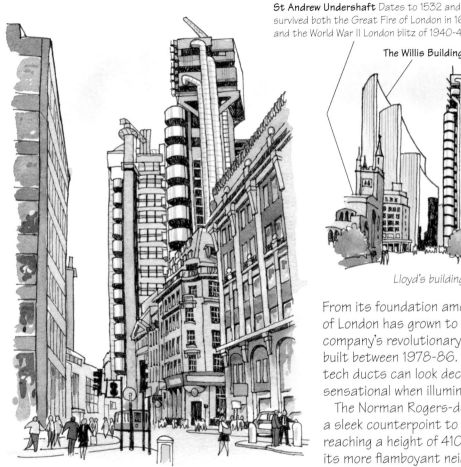

Lloyd's building from Cornhill

St Andrew Undershaft Dates to 1532 and survived both the Great Fire of London in 1666 and the World War II London blitz of 1940-41.

The Willis Building

Preserved façade of the original Lloyd's Insurance building.

Lloyd's building from St Mary Axe

The Monument from King William Street. (See page 71)

From its foundation amongst the 17th century coffee houses, Lloyd's of London has grown to become the world's premier insurer. The company's revolutionary building was designed by Richard Rogers and built between 1978-86. The stainless steel external piping and high-tech ducts can look deceptively ramshackle but the building looks sensational when illuminated at night.

The Norman Rogers-designed Willis Building, completed in 2008, is a sleek counterpoint to the Lloyds, curving seductively around it and reaching a height of 410ft (125m), around 100ft (30m) higher than its more flamboyant neighbour.

The Heron Tower at 110 Bishopsgate stands 755ft (230m) high, including its 92ft (28m) mast, currently the tallest building in the City of London. Designed by Kohn Pedersen Fox, it has a restaurant and sky bar on floors 32-40. There's also a 70,000 litre aquarium with sharks and 1,300 other fish.

30 St Mary Axe, affectionately known as 'The Gherkin', was designed by Norman Foster and opened in 2004. It has 40 floors and is 623ft (190m) high. The tower, London's first environmentally sustainable highrise, has a strange ethereal beauty, especially at night, and forms an almost surreal backdrop to the more traditional cityscapes.

St Ethelburga and the Gherkin

The Heron Tower under construction

One of the City's most striking buildings is also one of the oldest. St Ethelburga the Virgin dates from around 1400. It survived both the Great Fire and the World War II blitz but was almost destroyed by an IRA bomb in 1993. After an uncertain future, the elegant little church is now fully restored and a haven of human scale amongst the rather overbearing buildings along Bishopsgate.

St Botolph, Bishopsgate Dates to 1729 although there has been Christian worship on this site since Roman times. In 1993 an IRA bomb severely damaged many Bishopsgate buildings including St Botolph's. After extensive restoration the church was reopened in 1997.

Hackett Classic men's clothing

The White Hart

Bishopsgate at the junction with Liverpool Street

St Helen's Place off Bishopsgate

Once the site of a 16th century Benedictine Priory, St Helen's Place is a 1920s development now occupied by offices. A cathedral of modern office space, the Gherkin, intrudes into the elegant courtyard like an impudent teenager in a formal family photo.

ST PAUL'S

The great cathedral on Ludgate Hill dominates this area but there are several other notable places, both ancient and modern, that are well-worth visiting.

UNDERGROUND STATION   - - ▶ Suggested walking route

A walk of around 1.5 miles between St Paul's and Mansion House tube stations. Some gentle hills. Steps onto Southwark Bridge.

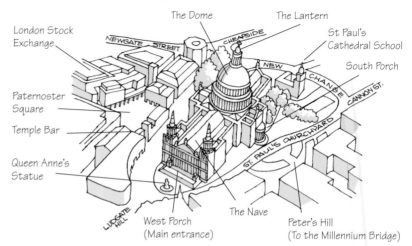

The Central Criminal court, commonly known as the Old Bailey, (from the street it stands in) opened in 1907 on the site of the notorious Newgate prison. Mass public hangings were held outside the gates until 1868. These days the Old Bailey deals with major criminal cases for the London area. The building dates from 1902 and is largely unremarkable, but the bronze statue on top of the dome, with the sword of strength in one hand and the scales of justice in the other, is world-famous.

Statue on the Old Bailey

St Paul's is the fifth cathedral to adorn Ludgate Hill, the first being a wooden building founded in 604. The fourth, largest in Britain, with a 149ft (489m) spire, was burnt to the ground in the Great Fire of 1666.

Sir Christopher Wren was commissioned to rebuild it, a task completed in 1710 when Wren was 78 years old and 35 years after the final design was agreed. Wren's initial Great Model of 1672 was unpopular with the authorities and what we see today is a watered-down compromise.

St Paul's famous dome was inspired by St Peter's Basilica in Rome, rising 365ft (108m) to the cross at its summit. The Whispering Gallery runs around the inside of the dome 99ft (30.2m) above the cathedral floor, reached by 259 steps from ground level. It's so named because a whisper against its wall is audible all round the gallery. The familiar twin towers at the western end were not part of Wren's original plans but he added them in 1707. Each was designed to hold a clock.

Inside, St Paul's is remarkably spacious, cool and well ordered. The Baroque splendour beneath the massive 102ft (31m) diameter dome has been the scene of many great national events, among them the funeral of Winston Churchill in 1965 and the wedding of Prince Charles and Lady Diana Spencer in 1981.

Ironically, a specially introduced coal tax funded the new cathedral, replacing the one destroyed by fire.

St Paul's Cathedral from Ludgate Hill

61

The steps of St Paul's are a favourite resting place for tourists, with a splendid view down Ludgate Hill, site of a gate to the City that was demolished with its attached gaol in 1780. A rail bridge which crossed the street for many years remained until 1990, when it was taken down to enable the construction of the City Thameslink railway station in a tunnel. A blue plaque near the bottom of the hill commemorates the publication nearby of London's first newspaper (*The Daily Courant*) in 1702.

Temple Bar

Queen Anne's statue An 1886 copy of Francis Bird's 1712 original.

St Martin, Ludgate Rebuilt in 1677-84 by Sir Christopher Wren

Ludgate Hill from the steps of St Paul's

The only surviving gateway into the City of London, Temple Bar has a chequered history. First erected by Charles II at the junction of Fleet Street and the Strand in 1671, the monument was taken down, stone by stone, in 1878 when it began to impede traffic flow. An alternative site elsewhere in the City couldn't be found so the brewer, Sir Henry Meux, acquired the stones In 1887 and rebuilt the Bar as the gateway to his estate in Hertfordshire.

Over the years it suffered vandalism and deterioration until, after a long campaign by the Temple Bar Trust, the Bar was returned to the City and finally reconstructed as a magnificent entrance to Paternoster Square in 2004.

PATERNOSTER SQUARE

During 1996-2003, William Whitfield's masterplan converted Paternoster Square from a rather grim 1960s eyesore adjacent to St Paul's into a bright and vibrant area of shops, offices and restaurants. A sympathetic backdrop to the majestic cathedral, the square is now home to the relocated London Stock Exchange and a number of other large financial organisations.

The main monument in the central piazza is the 75ft (23m) tall Paternoster Square Column, a Corinthian column of Portland stone topped by a flaming copper urn covered in gold leaf. It's illuminated by fibre-optic lighting at night and sometimes referred to as the 'pineapple'.

Development around St Paul's continues apace. Cheapside, once an undistinguished area east of the cathedral haphazardly rebuilt after the World War II bombing, has been revitalised with the 2010 opening of One New Change, a mammoth office and retail centre and the arrival of a spree of new shops and food outlets of the sort that used to be found only in the West End.

Meeting & greeting in Paternoster Square

Walkway alongside the Stock Exchange

'Shepherd and Sheep' by Dame Elisabeth Frink outside the Stock Exchange. Who's shepherding who?

63

THE MILLENNIUM BRIDGE

After a grand opening in 2000, pedestrians crossing the Millennium Bridge felt an unexpected swaying motion. The bridge was closed and Londoners instantly nicknamed it the 'Wobbly Bridge', ensuring its place in popular culture for evermore. Extensive modifications over the next two years followed, at an additional cost of £5 million. The bridge reopened in February 2002.

Now considered to be a great triumph, the handsome steel suspension bridge for pedestrians crosses the river from St Paul's to Tate Modern, providing some fabulous panoramic views along the way.

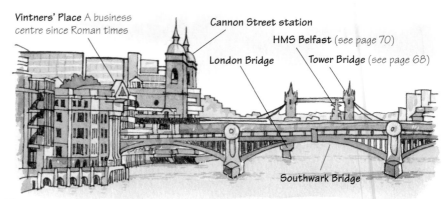

Vintners' Place A business centre since Roman times

Cannon Street station

HMS Belfast (see page 70)

London Bridge

Tower Bridge (see page 68)

Southwark Bridge

View east from Millennium Bridge

The view looking eastwards from the Millennium Bridge is particularly fine.

Southwark Bridge was opened in 1819. Notable for the centre arch, which at 240ft (73m) wide is the longest cast iron span ever made.

Cannon Street station was opened in 1886 to serve the south-east of England. The station's eight platforms now have office blocks built above them.

The current **London Bridge** was opened in 1973, the latest in a succession of river crossings at this point going back almost 2,000 years to the Roman occupation. The medieval version had 19 small arches and a drawbridge, and was crowded with buildings up to seven storeys high.

St Paul's Cathedral (See page 61)

City of London School

The Millennium Bridge

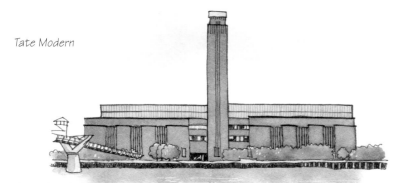

Tate Modern

Based in the former Bankside power station, Tate Modern is the most-visited modern art gallery in the world, with around 4.7 million visitors per year. The permanent collection consists of international works from 1900 onwards with several more galleries housing temporary exhibitions. The vast Turbine Hall is used to display large specially-commissioned works by contemporary artists, often generating popular media controversy.

Founded by the pioneering American actor and director Sam Wanamaker, Shakespeare's Globe is a unique reconstruction of Shakespeare's Elizabethan theatre on the southern bank of the Thames. It opened in 1997 and like the original, which burnt down in 1613, the centre of the circular structure is open to the elements, so public performances are restricted to the summer months.

Shakespeare's Globe

Crossing the Millennium Bridge to St Paul's

TOWER OF LONDON

Begun by William the Conqueror around the 1070s, The Tower of London is a large fortress used for various purposes over the centuries including a royal residence, a much-feared prison and an execution site. The Tower is a complex of several buildings set within two concentric rings of defensive walls and a moat. There were major expansions in the 12th and 13th centuries but the layout we see today is much as it was 700 years ago.

The Tower has been a tourist attraction since the reign of Charles II (1660-85) when the Crown Jewels were first put on display.

The oldest part of the Tower complex, the White Tower or the 'keep', was built as a residence for William I. He lived on the top floor, out of danger, with his court on the floors below. The walls of the White Tower are 15ft (4.6m) thick and rise to 90ft (27m) in height, making the castle the tallest building in London at the time. It was named the White Tower after being whitewashed in 1240. Today it holds a collection of arms and armour.

The Round Tower Once used as an observatory

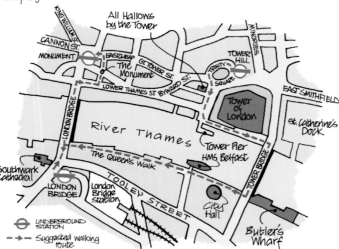

A walk of around two miles between Tower Hill and Monument tube stations. Some steps on and off the bridges.

The White Tower

The Tower has a long history of dark deeds, cruelty and death. For over 900 years, being 'sent to the Tower' was a fearful fate. Kept in appalling conditions, prisoners were often tortured before being executed on Tower Hill. Over 400 years, 112 people were executed there. Before the 20th century, there were seven executions within the castle on Tower Green, among them Anne Boleyn in 1536, Catherine Howard in 1542 and Lady Jane Grey in 1554.

The last ever prisoner was Hitler's deputy, Rudolph Hess, detained in the Tower for four days in 1941.

At least six ravens are kept at the Tower at all times, in the ancient belief that if they are absent the kingdom will fall. Dead ravens are honoured with their own memorial within the walls.

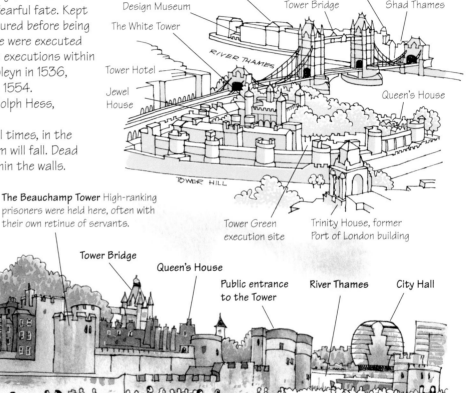

Jewel House Where the Crown Jewels are kept.

The White Tower

The Beauchamp Tower High-ranking prisoners were held here, often with their own retinue of servants.

Tower Bridge

Queen's House

Public entrance to the Tower

River Thames

City Hall

Tower Green execution site

Trinity House, former Port of London building

Tower of London panorama from the west

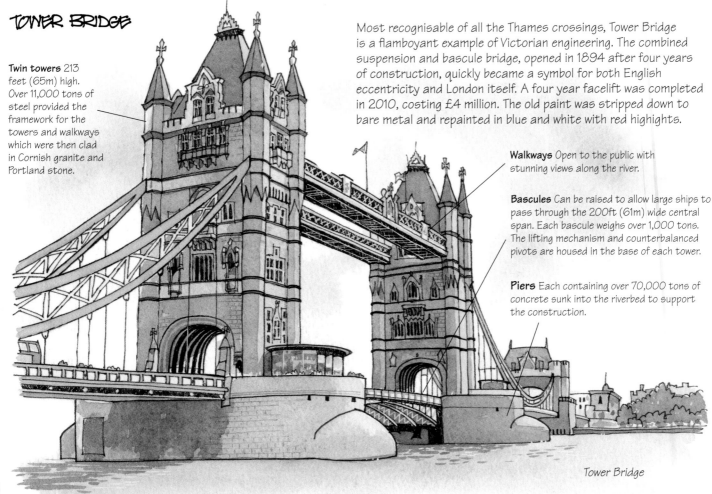

TOWER BRIDGE

Twin towers 213 feet (65m) high. Over 11,000 tons of steel provided the framework for the towers and walkways which were then clad in Cornish granite and Portland stone.

Most recognisable of all the Thames crossings, Tower Bridge is a flamboyant example of Victorian engineering. The combined suspension and bascule bridge, opened in 1894 after four years of construction, quickly became a symbol for both English eccentricity and London itself. A four year facelift was completed in 2010, costing £4 million. The old paint was stripped down to bare metal and repainted in blue and white with red highights.

Walkways Open to the public with stunning views along the river.

Bascules Can be raised to allow large ships to pass through the 200ft (61m) wide central span. Each bascule weighs over 1,000 tons. The lifting mechanism and counterbalanced pivots are housed in the base of each tower.

Piers Each containing over 70,000 tons of concrete sunk into the riverbed to support the construction.

Tower Bridge

Bascule opened to allow ship passage

The largely unchanging look of the ancient Tower seen from Tower Bridge contrasts vividly with that of the City beyond, where cranes gather in a seemingly endless competition to construct the most audacious building in the capital.

East of Tower Bridge, the south side of the Thames is edged by Butler's Wharf, once an important shipping wharf and warehouse, built in 1871-73, for goods unloaded from ships in the Port of London and containing what was then the largest tea warehouse in the world.

As the river trade declined during the 20th century, Butler's Wharf and other warehouses fell into disuse. However, since the 1980s they have been converted to luxury apartments, and the street behind them, renamed Shad Thames, transformed into a lively mix of trendy shops and restaurants with features of the old warehouses pleasingly incorporated.

All Hallows-by-the-Tower
Established in 675, the little church is 1,300 years old. Has a crypt museum, a Roman pavement and Roman and Saxon artifacts. John Quincy Adams, sixth President of the USA, was married here in 1797.

Minster Court, Mincing Lane
Completed between 1991-92 in a Postmodern-Gothic style. Appeared briefly in the film 101 Dalmations as house of De Vil.

Tower 42 (Originally the Nat West Tower) Opened in 1980. At 600ft (183m) high it was the tallest building in the City until 2010.

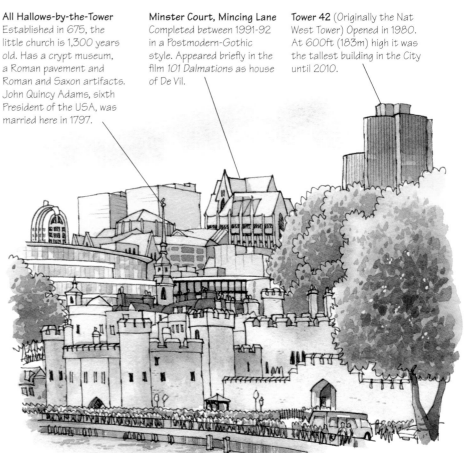

View to the City from Tower Bridge

BT Tower (completed in 1964) Situated in Cleveland Street, Fitzrovia. Has been previously known as the Post Office Tower, the London Telecom Tower and the British Telecom Tower. The main structure is 581ft (177m) tall, with a further section of aerial rigging bringing the total height to 620 ft (189m). Until the mid-1990s, the building was officially a secret and did not appear on official maps. Its existence was finally 'confirmed' by Kate Hoey, MP, in 1993. The tower is still in use as part of a major UK communications hub.

HMS Belfast Launched in Belfast in 1938. The Royal Navy light cruiser spent most of World War II protecting Atlantic convoys and took part in the Normandy landings in 1945. Saw further combat action in 1950-52 during the Korean War. After extensive modernisation during 1956-59 more foreign commissions followed before Belfast finally entered reserve in 1971. Saved from destruction by a trust formed in 1971, she was moored permanently on the Thames as a branch of the Imperial War Museum in 1978. A popular tourist attraction, Belfast receives around 250,000 visitors per year.

Anchor Brewhouse Once owned by Courage. Brewing began on this site in 1787. The building was converted to luxury apartments in 1985

Butler's Wharf

Shad Thames

Anchor Brewhouse from Tower Bridge

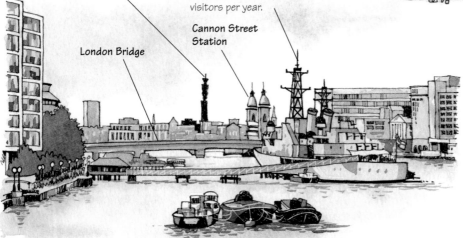

London Bridge

Cannon Street Station

The view west from Tower Bridge

City Hall is the headquarters of the Greater London Authority (GLA) which comprises the Mayor of London and the London Assembly. The landmark building was designed by Sir Norman Foster and opened in July 2002, two years after the Greater London Authority was created at a cost of £65 million. It's unusual, bulbous shape is intended to reduce the surface area and thus improve energy efficiency. The look of the edifice depends on where you're standing. From some angles City Hall looks terrific, from others it resembles a large, squashed pudding.

Southwark Cathedral

Southwark Cathedral, the mother church of the Anglican Diocese of Southwark, has been a place of Christian worship for over 1,000 years, but a cathedral only since 1905. The present building is mainly Gothic, dating from around 1220 to 1420, when the building was attached to a priory. Many of the medieval features remain.

The Monument is a 202ft (62m) tall, stone Roman Doric column crowned by a flaming urn of gilt bronze, commemorating the Great Fire of London which started in Pudding Lane, about 202ft (62m) away. Constructed between 1671 and 1677 and designed by Christopher Wren and Robert Hooke, it's the tallest isolated stone column in the world. The massive monolith stands on the site of St Margaret's, Fish Street, the first church to be burned down by the Great Fire. A viewing platform at the top is reached by a narrow winding staircase of 311 steps. The views are even more breath-taking than the climb.

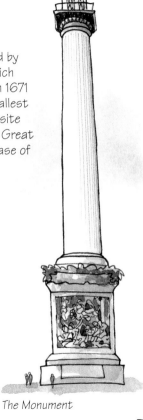

The Monument

City Hall from Tower Bridge

City Hall from across the Thames

71

CHELSEA

Originally a riverside village, Chelsea became fashionable in Tudor times and is now part of the ultra-fashionable Royal Borough of Kensington and Chelsea, with a wealthy population of bankers, IT whizz-kids and film stars.

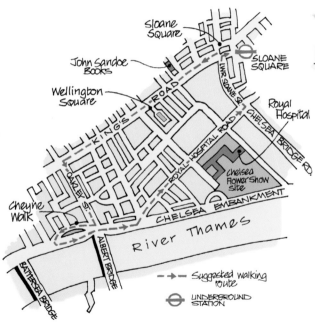

A circular walk of around two miles, beginning and ending at Sloane Square tube station.

Sloane Square

The wealth of Chelsea residents inspired the term 'Sloane Ranger', which usually refers to stereotypical upper class young women who share distinctive and common lifestyles, a particular archetype being Diana, Princess of Wales. Sloanes used to zip around in sports cars but in the mid 2000s switched to doing the school runs in 'Chelsea tractors', large 4x4 vehicles designed for off-road heavy duties.

Male Sloanes exist and have been referred to as 'Ra Ra Ruperts' (or, simply, Rah for short) and 'Hooray Henrys'. They are particularly well-known for their braying voices, most often heard in expensive bars and restaurants.

King's Road chic

The King's Road runs west for about two miles from Sloane Square. It's traditionally associated with 1960s style and fashion figures such as Mary Quant and Vivienne Westwood, and the Punk generation. Most of the counterculture has now been gentrified and a walk down the Kings Road these days is not a lot different from walking the High Street of any British town. Providing, of course, you ignore all the grand squares and streets leading off it.

The Queen's Head A traditional London pub.

Tryon Street, off the King's Road

The veteran Chelsea bookseller, John Sandoe, who died in 2007, sold the independent bookshop to members of staff in 1989. The much-loved, old-fashioned shop – once a grooming parlour for poodles – is a cornucopia of 25,000 books, groaning shelves and narrow steps, and counts Elton John and Tom Stoppard amongst its many celebrity shoppers.

Wellington Square

John Sandoe Books, Blacklands Terrace

One of a number of fashionable squares off the King's Road, Wellington Square was completed in 1852, coinciding with the death of the Duke of Wellington, hero of Waterloo. His body was brought to Chelsea Hospital for lying in state, inspiring the square's name. The elegant stucco houses have iron first floor railings and there are Ionic porches over some front doors. The author of Winnie the Pooh, A.A. Milne, lived in the square and it's said to be the fictious home of James Bond.

Parts of Chelsea are still redolent of the 'Swinging Sixties' and don't look much different today. Mick Jagger and Marianne Faithfull lived at No 48 Cheyne Walk from 1967 to 1978 and Keith Richards at No 3. The footballer, George Best, had a flat in the area and the cartoonist, Gerald Scarfe, scourge of 1960s politicians, still lives in Cheyne Walk. A pink doorway in Oakley Street asserts that 'Love' still lives.

No 48 Cheyne Walk

No 3 Cheyne Walk

A typical Cheyne Walk Bentley

Before the construction of the Embankment in the 19th century, the houses along Cheyne Walk fronted the River Thames. It's now one of London's most classy addresses, boasting some of the capital's finest houses and attracting the rich and famous to buy the most sought-after homes with river views. Even the Thames has desirable property, with a flotilla of houseboats at Chelsea Wharf near Albert Bridge. One of those can cost up to £500,000 plus a mooring fee of around £50,000. The former Chelsea Art College now houses ultra-expensive flats where a parking space alone can cost £100,000.

As bridges go, Albert Bridge has never quite made it. Originally designed and built by Rowland Mason Ordish in 1873, it soon proved to be structurally unsound. A redesign in the late 1800s and another in 1973 resulted in an unusual hybrid of three different design styles.

Built as a toll bridge, it was also commercially unsuccessful. Six years after opening it was taken into public ownership and the tolls were lifted. The toll booths remained in place however, and are the only surviving examples of bridge toll booths in London.

Albert Bridge

The toll booths on Albert Bridge

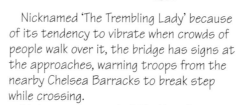

Nicknamed 'The Trembling Lady' because of its tendency to vibrate when crowds of people walk over it, the bridge has signs at the approaches, warning troops from the nearby Chelsea Barracks to break step while crossing.

With a roadway only 27ft (8.2m) wide and with serious structural weaknesses, it's also ill-equipped to cope with modern vehicular traffic. Some 20,000 vehicles cross every day.

In 1992, the Albert Bridge was rewired and painted in an unusual colour scheme designed to make it more conspicuous in poor visibility and less vulnerable to damage from shipping.

But despite all its shortcomings as a bridge, when it's illuminated by 4,000 bulbs at night, the Albert Bridge is one of West London's most striking landmarks.

King Charles II commissioned the elegant buildings of the Royal Hospital from Christopher Wren in 1682 as a retirement and nursing home for British soldiers unfit for further duty due to injury or old age, and who have no family to support them. Now universally and affectionately known as 'Chelsea pensioners', a cheery group of former soldiers in their famous red coats are regularly seen at national events such as the annual Remembrance Service in the Royal Albert Hall. The hospital is still home to some 400 pensioners who receive board and lodging, a uniform and nursing care. The extensive grounds are open to the public, along with some of the hospital buildings, and since 1913 have been the venue for the Royal Horticultural Society's world-famous Chelsea Flower Show.

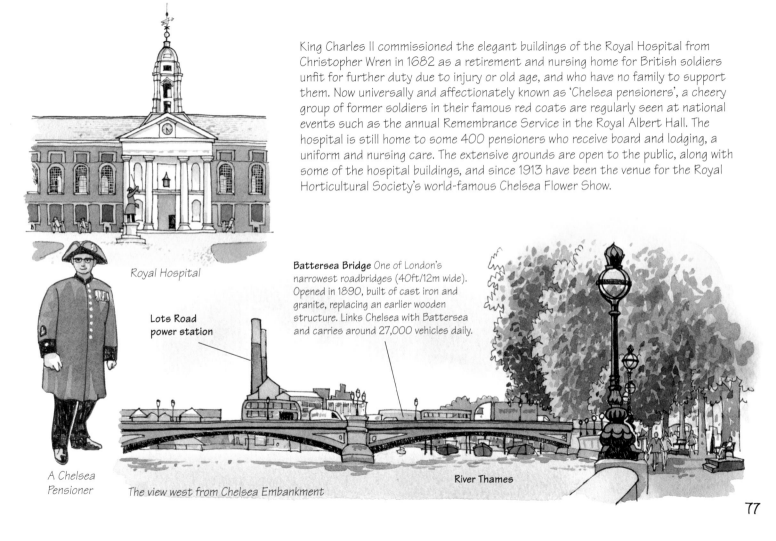

Royal Hospital

A Chelsea Pensioner

Lots Road power station

Battersea Bridge One of London's narrowest roadbridges (40ft/12m wide). Opened in 1890, built of cast iron and granite, replacing an earlier wooden structure. Links Chelsea with Battersea and carries around 27,000 vehicles daily.

The view west from Chelsea Embankment

River Thames

The map shows:

MARBLE ARCH
OXFORD ST.
Marble Arch
BAYSWATER ROAD
NORTH CARRIAGE ROAD
Speakers Corner
PARK LANE
BROAD WALK
Hyde Park
Kensington Gardens
The Serpentine
Diana, Princess of Wales, Memorial Fountain
The Lido
ROTTEN ROW
Albert Memorial
KENSINGTON ROAD
KNIGHTSBRIDGE
QUEENS GATE
EXHIBITION ROAD
Royal College of Music
Royal Albert Hall
Victoria & Albert Museum
BROMPTON ROAD
Harrods
Natural History Museum
UNDERGROUND STATION
Suggested walking route
SOUTH KENSINGTON

A walk of around three miles from Knightsbridge to Marble Arch tube stations.

KNIGHTSBRIDGE

Notable as an ultra-expensive residential area and for the number of its upmarket retail outlets, famously Harrods and Harvey Nichols, Knightsbridge is home to many of the world's richest people and has some of the highest property prices to match. A four-bedroomed apartment can cost over £25 million. Fourteen out of the top 200 most expensive streets in Britain are in Knightsbridge. The district is surprisingly leafy, especially so considering its location at the heart of London. It also has Britain's largest collection of museums – actually in neighbouring South Kensington – gathered together near Hyde Park as a result of the Great Exhibition in 1851.

Street restaurant, Brompton Road

Founded in 1852, The Victoria and Albert Museum (usually abbreviated as the V&A) is the world's largest museum of decorative arts and design, housing a permanent collection of over 4.5 million objects. Its collection spans 5,000 years, from ancient times to the present day, in virtually every medium.

Harrods department store

Wholesale grocer Charles Henry Harrod established his Knightsbridge shop in 1849. Harrods is now the world's largest store, occupying a five acre site with over a million square feet of retail space and some 330 departments.

Mohammed Al Fayed and his brother bought the store for £615 million in 1985 and sold it to the Qatari Royal Family for £1.5 billion in 2010, the year Harrods broke through the £1 billion annual sales target.

Main entrance to the V&A

The Natural History Museum is one of three large museums on Exhibition Road (the others are the Science Museum and the V&A). A treasure trove of life and earth sciences, it houses some 70 million items within five main collections: Botany, Entomology, Mineralogy, Palaeontology and Zoology, including specimens collected by Charles Darwin. Boring it isn't, with state of the art interactive displays and dinosaurs brought roaringly back to life with impressive animatronic models. Opened in 1881, the vast museum building is a masterwork in itself, designed by Alfred Waterhouse in his own idiosyncratic Romanesque style and making extensive use of decorated terracotta tiles to resist the sooty climate of Victorian London.

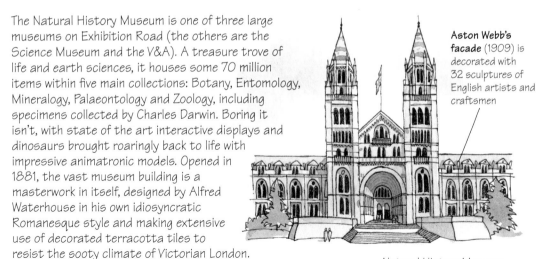

Aston Webb's facade (1909) is decorated with 32 sculptures of English artists and craftsmen

Natural History Museum

ROYAL ALBERT HALL

Recognisable the world over, the Royal Albert Hall is one of the UK's most treasured and distinctive buildings. Since its opening by Queen Victoria in 1871, the world's leading artists from every kind of genre have appeared here. Each year the hall hosts more than 350 performances, from classical and rock concerts, to community events and lavish banquets.

Designed by an engineer, Francis Fowke, the hall is an elliptical shape with a major axis of 272ft (83m). The great glass and wrought-iron domed roof is 135 ft (41m) high. Originally designed to hold 8,000 people, modern safety restrictions limit the maximum capacity to 5,544. A great mosaic frieze, depicting 'The Triumph of Arts and Sciences', runs around the outside.

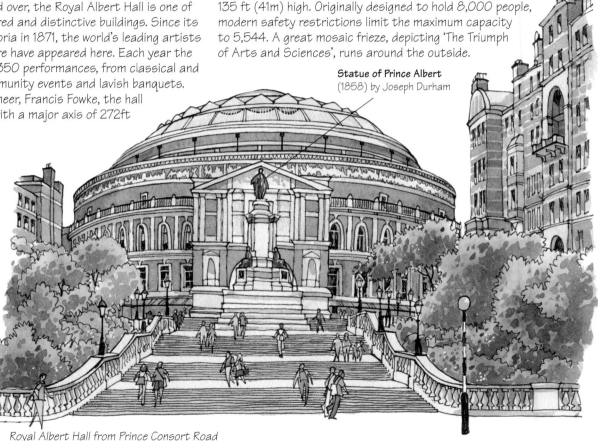

Statue of Prince Albert
(1858) by Joseph Durham

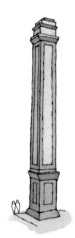

An industrial sized chimney on the west side of the building was built around 1885 to vent the Hall's boilers and is still in use today.

Royal Albert Hall from Prince Consort Road

80

Set opposite the Albert Hall on the edge of Hyde Park, the Albert Memorial was commissioned by Queen Victoria in memory of her beloved husband, Prince Albert, who died of typhoid in 1861. The memorial was designed by Sir George Gilbert Scott in an extravagent Gothic Revival style and opened in 1872 by the Queen.

Matching the Queen's grief, the memorial is on a massive scale, 176ft (54m) tall and taking over ten years to complete, at a cost of £120,000 (about £10 million today) met by public subscription.

The centrepiece is a seated figure of Prince Albert beneath a canopy – said to have been inspired by a medieval town cross – elaborately decorated with multi-coloured marble, stones, mosaics, enamels, wrought iron and nearly 200 sculpted figures. Restrained, it isn't.

Albert Memorial

Royal College of Music

The Royal College of Music was founded by Royal Charter in 1882. The College's impressive red brick building was designed by Sir Arthur Blomfield in Flemish Mannerist style and built in 1892-94.

For eighty years Albert's statue was covered in black 'paint' thought to have been deliberately applied during World War I to prevent it becoming a target for Zeppelin bombing raids or domestic anti-German sentiment. However, modern research prior to a extensive restoration during the 1980's suggests that the black coating was probably due to atmospheric pollution destroying the original gold leaf.

81

HYDE PARK

The largest of London's Royal Parks, Hyde Park covers 275 acres. Combined with adjoining Kensington Gardens it adds up to 625 acres of open parkland – bigger than Monaco – in the centre of the most populous city in Europe.

The park was originally land which Henry VIII seized at the Dissolution of the Monasteries in 1536 and made his private hunting ground. James I opened it to the public in 1637 and the area became a prized public space, which in its time has been a venue for duels, horse racing, highwaymen, demonstrations, rock concerts and parades.

In 1730, Caroline, the queen of George II, dammed the Westbourne River to create the narrow and twisting Serpentine, a relatively shallow lake with a maximum depth of 40ft (12m), which divides the park in two.

The Great Exhibition of 1851 was held here, for which Joseph Paxton designed the Crystal Palace, a large exhibition hall, later moved to a site on Sydenham Hill where it was destroyed by fire in 1936.

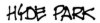

Broad Walk near Speakers Corner

Serpentine Bridge, which marks the boundary with Kensington Gardens

MARBLE ARCH

John Nash designed the white marble arch in 1827 as the entrance to Buckingham Palace, which he was upgrading at the time. Too narrow for the grandest of coaches to pass through, it was brought here in 1851 as a corner piece for Hyde Park, close to the site of the old Tyburn gallows where public hangings were held in front of baying crowds until 1783. Also nearby is Speakers Corner where budding orators can speak on whatever topic they like to similarly vocal modern audiences.

Park Lane apartments

← Bayswater Road   ↑ Great Cumberland Place   Oxford Street →

Once one of the capital's classiest addresses and still a valuable acquisition on a UK Monopoly board, Park Lane's appeal as a residential location was severely reduced during the 1960s, when the road, which runs for around three quarters of a mile between Hyde Park Corner and Marble Arch, was turned into a noisy, three-lane highway. However, Park Lane remains well upmarket, with a number of five-star hotels and – appropriately – several sports car showrooms.

BLOOMSBURY

The area has long been associated with literature, art and learning. The famous Bloomsbury Group of writers and artists met in private homes here during the 1930s and the area still boasts the University of London, the British Museum, the Royal Academy of Dramatic Art and several fine Georgian squares.

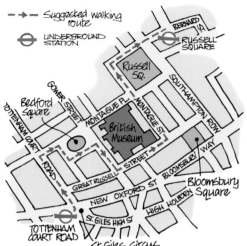

A walk of around 1.25 miles from Tottenham Court Road to Russell Square tube stations.

Bedford Square. A good place to sit and put the world to rights.

The Bloomsbury area was developed by the Russell family during the 17th and 18th centuries, turning what was described in the 1086 Domesday Book as having vineyards and 'wood for 100 pigs', into a fashionable residential area.

Bedford Square was built 1775-83 and is one of the best preserved set pieces of Georgian architecture in London. Most of the houses have been turned into offices but the many beautiful doorways are unaltered.

Bedford Square doorways

BRITISH MUSEUM

British Museum

Museum Street, opposite the museum, dates back to the 14th century, and today is an attractive collection of small shops, bookshops and cafes, well-worth exploring. There's even a traditional 17th century pub (Museum Tavern) on the corner, which serves pub grub but is untainted by games machines, TV or any other modern intrusions.

Animated clock in Museum Street

Bloomsbury's greatest treasure is the British Museum, the world's oldest public museum, established in 1753 to house the collection of the physician Sir Hans Sloane. Since then it has grown to more than seven million objects, originating from all continents, which illustrate and document the story of human culture from its beginnings to the present. Like all other national museums in the United Kingdom, it charges no admission fee.

The 1850s façade facing Great Russell Street is a characteristic building of Sir Robert Smirke, with 44 Ionic columns 45ft (14m) high, closely based on the ancient temples of Greece. Architecturally, the building was hauled into the 21st century with the addition in 2000 of Norman Foster's Great Court with the famous old reading room at its centre.

Museum Tavern, Great Russell Street

Russell Square Garden

Originally developed by the Dukes of Bedford during the 17th and 18th centuries, Russell Square contained large terraced houses aimed mainly at upper middle class families. A number survive along the southern and western sides. In 2002, the square was re-landscaped, returning the garden to its original early 19th century layout by Humphry Repton, and a modern fountain added. The four-star Hotel Russell, opened in 1898, dominates the northern corner of the square.

Opened in 1906, Russell Square tube station has no escalators, just three lifts and a spiral staircase of 177 steps.

The station became news on 7th July, 2005, when a bomb exploded on a train from King's Cross killing 26 people, the largest loss of life from four coordinated suicide attacks across London that morning. The first two were on tube trains from Liverpool Street to Aldgate and Edgeware Road to Paddington. The final explosion occurred on a bus in Tavistock Square.

A total of 52 people were killed and some 700 injured. The four bombers also died.

Russell Square tube station

MARYLEBONE

The medieval village of Marylebone (from Maryburne – the stream by St Mary's) lies south of Regent's Park. The area now has London's largest concentration of Georgian houses, Nash terraces and the capital's busiest park.

Madame Tussauds, the museum of wax figures of famous people, is housed in two of the capital's most unlovely buildings. The domed one was originally the London Planetarium, opened in 1958. It became part of Madame Tussauds in 2006 and is now part of its exhibition area.

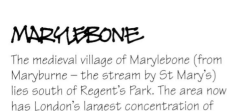

Madame Tussauds

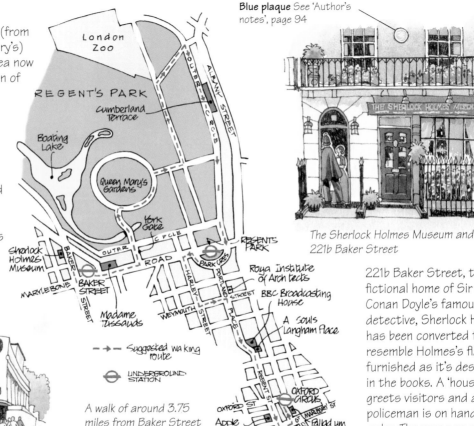

Blue plaque See 'Author's notes', page 94

The Sherlock Holmes Museum and 221b Baker Street

A walk of around 3.75 miles from Baker Street to Oxford Circus tube stations.

221b Baker Street, the fictional home of Sir Arthur Conan Doyle's famous detective, Sherlock Holmes, has been converted to resemble Holmes's flat, furnished as it's described in the books. A 'housekeeper' greets visitors and a period policeman is on hand to keep order. The museum on the ground floor sells Holmes memorabilia.

REGENT'S PARK

Queen Mary's Gardens, Regent's Park

The 410 acres of Regent's Park enjoy a wide range of facilities and amenities including gardens; a lake with a heronry, waterfowl and a boating area; sports pitches and children's playgrounds. Queen Mary's Gardens is the most carefully tended part. Regent's Canal curves along one side and London Zoo occupies the northern end.

Cumberland Terrace

Most of the west side of the park is lined with elegant white stucco terraces of houses designed by John Nash. Completed in 1826, Cumberland Terrace consists of three main blocks, linked together by decorative arches with typical neoclassical style and grandeur. The central block includes a large sculptural pediment above a long colonnade of Ionic columns. The Terrace remains in residential use. It originally comprised 31 houses but parts of it have now been converted into grand apartments.

John Nash's elegant grand design extends south of Regent's Park to the
beautiful curve of Park Crescent, a stuccoed semicircular terrace of houses
completed in 1821. Many are now converted into expensive apartments.

Harley Street has been well-known for private
medicine since the 19th century. Today, some 3,000
people are employed in the area's clinics, medical
and paramedical practices, and hospitals such as
The London Clinic. Many famous people have lived in
Harley Street, including the Victorian prime minister
William Gladstone and the artist J.M.W. Turner.

Park Crescent

Harley Street doorways

Regent Street

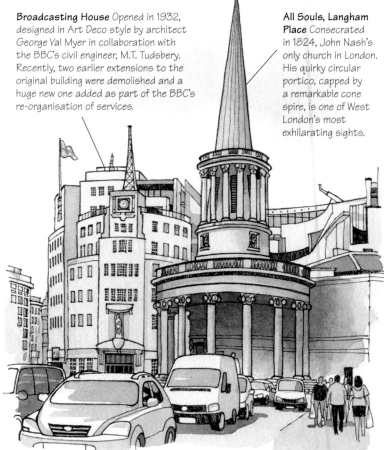

Broadcasting House Opened in 1932, designed in Art Deco style by architect George Val Myer in collaboration with the BBC's civil engineer, M.T. Tudsbery. Recently, two earlier extensions to the original building were demolished and a huge new one added as part of the BBC's re-organisation of services.

All Souls, Langham Place Consecrated in 1824, John Nash's only church in London. His quirky circular portico, capped by a remarkable cone spire, is one of West London's most exhilarating sights.

Broadcasting House & All Souls, Langham Place

Named after the Prince Regent (later George IV), Regent Street is one of the West End's major shopping areas, well-known to tourists and Londoners alike and famous for its Christmas decorations. Completed in 1825, the street was part of John Nash's processional route to link the Prince's residence at Carlton House in St James's with Regent's Park.

Regent Street ends abruptly in a dogleg to align it with the pre-existing Portland Place. The bend is strikingly filled by Broadcasting House, flagship of the BBC, and All Souls church, the only surviving Nash building in the street.

London Palladium, Argyll Street

London's most famous variety theatre, the 2,286 seater London Palladium opened in 1910. Between 1955-67 it was the venue for the top-rated ITV show *Sunday Night at the London Palladium*, broadcast live across the nation every week and featuring top UK and American acts.

The Apple Store in Regent Street was the first to open in Europe in November 2004. It is said to be the most profitable shop in London with the highest sales per square foot, taking £60 million a year, or £2,000 per square foot.

Apple Store, Regent Street

Liberty store, Regent Street

Arthur Lasenby Liberty opened his first shop on Regent Street in 1875, selling oriental silks and *objets d'art* from Japan. The present mock Tudor building was built specifically to house the store in 1925. Liberty is one of the leading destination stores in London, a wonderful emporium where the latest fashions sit alongside design classics.

RAILWAY STATIONS

Trains from Liverpool Street Station go to Stansted Airport and Norfolk. There's been a station here since 1874. It was extensively updated in 1985 and again in 1992 when the platforms in the main shed were lined up and a new underground booking office built. The façade and Victorian cast-iron pillars inside were retained. It's now impressively clean and tidy, looking more like a supermarket than a railway station.

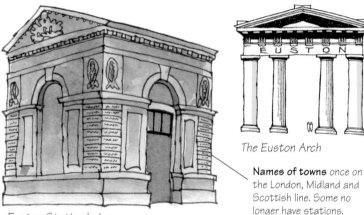

Euston Station lodge

The Euston Arch

Names of towns once on the London, Midland and Scottish line. Some no longer have stations.

Liverpool Street Station

The original Euston Station was opened in 1837 with a 72ft (22m) high Doric entrance arch, the largest ever built. By 1960 the old building had become unsuitable for modern requirements so, amid much public outcry, the station, including the Euston Arch, was demolished.

Its rather bland replacement opened in 1968 serving the newly electrified West Coast main line. Two stone lodges which stood either side of the great arch remain, a poignant reminder of glory lost.

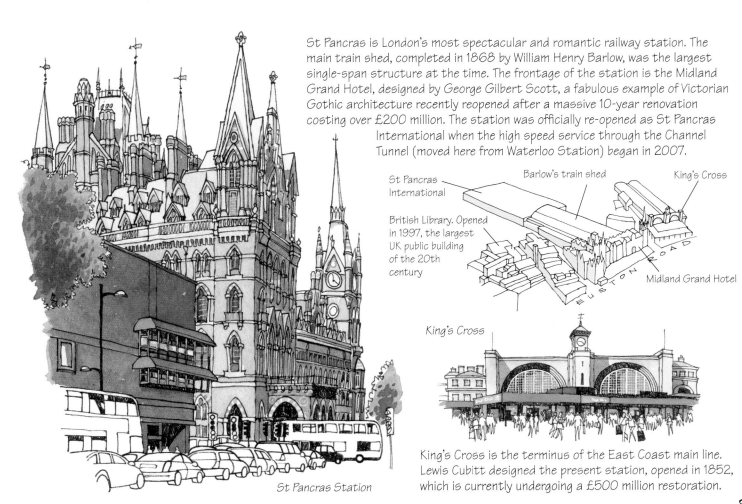

St Pancras is London's most spectacular and romantic railway station. The main train shed, completed in 1868 by William Henry Barlow, was the largest single-span structure at the time. The frontage of the station is the Midland Grand Hotel, designed by George Gilbert Scott, a fabulous example of Victorian Gothic architecture recently reopened after a massive 10-year renovation costing over £200 million. The station was officially re-opened as St Pancras International when the high speed service through the Channel Tunnel (moved here from Waterloo Station) began in 2007.

St Pancras International

Barlow's train shed

King's Cross

British Library. Opened in 1997, the largest UK public building of the 20th century

EUSTON ROAD

Midland Grand Hotel

King's Cross

St Pancras Station

King's Cross is the terminus of the East Coast main line. Lewis Cubitt designed the present station, opened in 1852, which is currently undergoing a £500 million restoration.

93

AUTHOR'S NOTES

Black cabs

An institution almost as familiar as the red buses, motorised hackney cabs in London are traditionally all black, although they are now painted in a variety of colours, sometimes in advertising brand liveries. The capital has around 21,000 black cabs, each carrying up to five passengers. Cab drivers have to pass a test called *The Knowledge* to demonstrate they have an intimate knowledge of London's streets.

Blue plaques

Attached to buildings once occupied, sometimes fleetingly, by well-known people, virtuous or otherwise. The scheme began in 1867 with one for Lord Byron and is now run by English Heritage who receive about 100 viable suggestions a year. Only a handful make it through the selection process. The people commemorated don't necessarily have to existed – the plaque on 221b Baker Street (to Sherlock Holmes), for example – and sometimes they produce some odd bedfellows. A plaque for Handel in Brook Street has one next door for Jimi Hendrix.

Buses

The famous red Routemaster buses have been largely superseded but their replacements are also the familiar red colour. London's bus network is one of the largest in the world, running

Chelsea

24 hours a day, with 8,000 buses, 700 routes, and over 6 million passenger journeys made every weekday. In 2003, the network's ridership was estimated at over 1.5 billion passenger trips per annum, more than the Underground.

The City

Also known as 'The Square Mile'. Geographically it's the area first settled by the Roman invaders in AD 43. They built the first bridge over the Thames and named what was to become the capital, 'Londinium'. Some features of the ancient walled city persist and today's City is still in many ways separate from the rest of the capital. It has its own mayor and police force and, unlike the rest of the capital, which is divided into 32 boroughs, the City of London stands alone. 'The City' also refers to the centre of the UK's financial services.

Cockney

Traditionally a native of East London, born within the sound of the bells at St Mary-le-Bow church on Cheapside.

Some cockneys speak using cockney rhyming slang. This involves replacing the common word with a phrase of two or three words, and then in almost all cases, omitting the original rhyming word,

'Toilette', South Kensington

making the origin and meaning of the phrase elusive to non-cockney listeners. The most familiar use involves the replacement of 'stairs' with the rhyming 'apples and pears'. Following the pattern of omission, this would then be used only as 'apples'. Thus the spoken phrase 'I'm going up the apples' would mean 'I'm going upstairs'.

Cockneys usually speak quickly and combined with rhyming slang with sometimes double or even treble meanings it's a language all of its own and often incomprehensible beyond their own circle.

The Great Fire

Started at a baker's shop in Pudding Lane in September 1666. The fire raged for five days, finally engulfing an area reaching from close to the Tower of London to as far west as Fetter Lane. It consumed more than 13,000 houses – the homes of 85% of the City's population – 87 churches and St Paul's Cathedral. Only a handful of deaths were recorded. A year earlier the Plague had swept through London killing 100,000 people. It's thought that the fire destroyed many of the insanitary conditions which contributed to the Plague.

London Blitz

The sustained bombing of London by Nazi Germany during World War II. It began in September 1940, and nightly raids by up to 200 aircraft continued for two months. Over 20,000 civilians were killed and more than a million houses were destroyed or damaged. Londoners sheltered from the bombing in the underground stations and as far as possible normal life continued. People went to work, milk was delivered and the buses still ran, demonstrating the much vaunted 'spirit that won the war' attitude.

London was not the only city to suffer Luftwaffe bombing. Other important military and industrial centres throughout Britain suffered heavy air raids and high numbers of casualties.

London Underground

Also known as the 'Tube', it's the oldest and largest underground railway in the world, with the first section opened in 1863. It now has some 500 trains, around 250 miles of track and over 270 stations handling over three million passenger journeys on an average weekday.

There are many other transport alternatives throughout the capital, but for the purposes of the suggested walking routes in this book the tube is the fastest and most convenient way to get around. However, try and avoid the morning and evening rush hours. You can buy a Oyster card or Travelcard which provide discount fares and there's no queuing for a ticket on each journey.

Pearly Kings and Queens

The practice of wearing clothes decorated with pearl buttons originated in the 19th century. At the time,

Shops, Fleet Street

'Costermongers' (London street traders) were in the habit of wearing pearl buttons along the seams of their trousers. Henry Croft, an orphan street sweeper who collected money for charity, adapted this to create the 'pearly suit' to draw attention to himself and aid his fund-raising activities. In 1911, an organised Pearly Society was formed in Finchley, North London, and continues the charity tradition today.

River Thames

From its source in the Cotswolds, the River Thames flows for 215 miles to its outflow into the North Sea at Southend-on-Sea, Essex. The section through London is tidal, with a rise and fall of about seven feet.

The riverbanks along an approximately five-mile stretch through central London are lined with historical references and a river cruise is an excellent way to see them. Passenger boat services cover about 30 miles of the Thames, from Hampton Court in the west to the Thames Barrier in the east.

The Annual Boat Race – a uniquely British occasion – takes place every spring, when rowing eights representing Cambridge and Oxford universities race between Putney and Mortlake watched by a TV audience of millions, the majority of whom usually have no interest at all in rowing.

LONDON...

★ is the largest metropolitan area in the UK.

★ is the largest urban zone in the EU.

★ is home to the headquarters of more than 100 of Europe's 500 largest companies.

★ is the most visited city in the world.

★ has five international airports.

★ has the busiest airspace in the world.

★ in 2012 will become the first city to host the Summer Olympics three times. (Previously in 1908 and 1948).

★ is Europe's most racially and culturally diverse city.

★ has more than 300 languages spoken.

★ has a population of 7.5 million within the boundaries of Greater London.

★ is the most populous municipality in the EU.

★ contains four World Heritage Sites: the Tower of London, Kew Gardens, Westminster and Greenwich.

★ has over 40 theatres.

★ generates approximately 20 per cent of the United Kingdom's GDP.

★ is the second-largest port in the UK, handling 53 million tonnes of cargo each year.

★ is home to five major medical schools.

★ has thirteen League football clubs, five in the Premier League: Arsenal, Chelsea, Fulham, Tottenham Hotspur and West Ham United.

★ sets the world's time at Greenwich.

Also in the Sketchbook series...

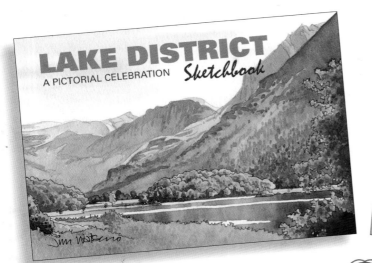

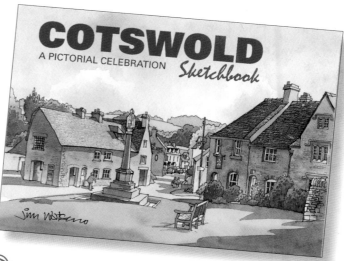

SURVIVAL BOOKS
www.survivalbooks.net

A tour of favourite Lake District towns, villages, lakes and dales, packed with colour illustrations, history, facts and figures, and some quirky surprises. The perfect guidebook, gift or souvenir.

All you need to enjoy visiting 37 Cotswold towns and villages. Packed with colour illustrations and history, plus facts and figures, and some quirky surprises. The perfect guidebook, gift or souvenir.

Celebrating the most beautiful regions of Britain